Study Guide

50 Ways to Improve Student Behavior

Simple Solutions to Complex Challenges

Annette Breaux and Todd Whitaker

D1318381

EYE ON EDUCATION
6 DEPOT WAY WEST, SUITE 106
LARCHMONT, NY 10538
(914) 833-0551
(914) 833-0761 fax
www.eyeoneducation.com

10 9 8 7 6 5 4 3 2

Editorial and production services provided by
Hypertext Book and Journal Services
738 Saltillo St., San Antonio, TX 78207-6953 (210-227-6055)

Table of Contents

Introduction

This *Study Guide* has been developed to accompany the book *50 Ways to Improve Student Behavior: Simple Solutions to Complex Challenges* by Annette Breaux and Dr. Todd Whitaker. It offers questions and prompts to enable readers to interact with the book's content. Each of the 50 solutions and strategies in the *Study Guide* are organized into three sections: What Is, What Could Be, and Make it Real. The exercises and questions in the Study Guide provide opportunities for readers to master the concepts in the book and to apply them in their own classrooms.

The authors would like to thank Dr. Lolli Haws, Principal of Oakridge Elementary School in Arlington, Virginia, for the contributions she made in the preparation of this Study Guide.

—Annette Breaux and Todd Whitaker

Meet and Greet:
Classroom Solution/Strategy #1

Students who feel welcome and are greeted warmly are more likely to want to be in your class!

What is:

Consider your current classroom environment. What three things are you already doing to make your students feel welcome and wanted?

1. _____
2. _____
3. _____

Rate yourself for creating a warm and welcoming atmosphere in your classroom:

Seriously Lacking   Room for Improvement   Good   Excellent

What thoughts do you have about the rating you gave yourself?

_____
_____
_____

What could be:

Greeting each student personally each day is **important**! Practice this skill by writing 10 personalized greetings you could use with your students tomorrow. Make sure they are individualized and personal. Hint: Share your 10 with 3 colleagues and you'll have a list with as many as 30 possible greetings!

1. _____
2. _____
3. _____
4. _____

5. _____

6. _____

7. _____

8. _____

9. _____

10. _____

What changes might you see in your students if you greeted them each day?

_____

_____

_____

_____

Name three of your most challenging, unmotivated, or unruly students. Create two personalized greetings for each of those students.

Name: _____

   Greeting 1: _____

   Greeting 2: _____

Name: _____

   Greeting 1: _____

   Greeting 2: _____

Name: _____

   Greeting 1: _____

   Greeting 2: _____

Make it real:

Greet your students warmly and personally every day for a week. Note any differences in behavior, tone, and attitude in your students and in yourself.

_____

_____

Letter of Introduction: Classroom Solution/Strategy #2

Writing a welcome letter helps you establish a positive relationship with your students and their parents.

What is:

What strategies do you already use to establish a positive relationship with your new students and their parents at the start of every year or semester? (Open House Night activities? Written communication? Welcome messages in the classroom?)

1. _____
2. _____
3. _____

What could be:

The authors suggested the content for a letter (or postcard) to students or parents. Write your own student letter or message below:

_____
_____
_____
_____
_____

Write your own parent letter or message below:

_____
_____
_____
_____
_____

Consider all the possibilities. What alternative means could you use to welcome students and get to know them?

Describe your own "welcome" or "get to know you" activity below:

_____

_____

_____

_____

_____

_____

Share your ideas with a group of colleagues. Then you will all have several new ways to welcome your students and get to know them from day one!

Name one strategy you currently use to foster positive relationships with parents.

_____

_____

_____

Share the strategy you just listed with several colleagues and have them share theirs with you.

Make it real:

Are lots of ideas flowing now? Outline a plan for how you will start the new school year or semester with a strong relationship-building introductory activity.

_____

_____

_____

How can you build on the new introductory strategies you employed in August/ September throughout the year? Remember to keep the relationships strong all year long.

_____

_____

_____

Tools for Rules and Procedures: Classroom Solution/Strategy #3

Know the difference between rules and procedures. Practice procedures and establish consequences for broken rules.

What is:

List five of your current classroom rules as they are stated now:

1. _____
2. _____
3. _____
4. _____
5. _____

List up to five procedures you currently use to keep your classroom organized and running smoothly.

1. _____
2. _____
3. _____
4. _____
5. _____

What could be:

Procedures: How do they differ from rules?

_____
_____
_____
_____

Look at your list of five rules and procedures above. Do they need to be stated more clearly? Have you mistakenly listed procedures as rules? Make any necessary corrections.

From the list below, circle three procedures which you currently don't use but feel you should.

- Turning in homework
- Use of classroom library
- Coming into the classroom
- Organizing desks or materials in desks
- Talking during group time
- Getting the teacher's attention
- Pencil sharpening
- How to obtain a restroom pass
- What to do when not feeling well
- During independent time, how to get help from the teacher (go to teacher, raise hand, etc.)
- Using computer time
- How to move to work stations
- What to do when the dismissal bell rings
- Getting permission to go to the library
- What to do if there is a substitute teacher

Other: _____   Other: _____

Other: _____   Other: _____

Other: _____   Other: _____

Rules: How do they differ from procedures?

_____

_____

_____

_____

Share your thoughts with two colleagues.

Make it real:

Write the details for five key procedures you will establish and discuss the steps you will follow to implement each.

1. Procedure: _____

   Steps: _____

2. Procedure: _____

   Steps: _____

3. Procedure: _____

   Steps: _____

4. Procedure: _____

   Steps: _____

5. Procedure: _____

   Steps: _____

Develop five basic classroom rules that you feel will adequately address potentially serious infractions. Share with two other colleagues. Ask them to recall several tough behaviors they have encountered and see if one of your rules applies!

Rule #1: _____

Rule #2: _____

Rule #3: _____

Rule #4: _____

Rule #5: _____

Consequences:
List your planned consequences for breaking classroom rules below:

1. _____

2. _____

3. _____

4. _____

5. _____

Are You All Right?
Classroom Solution/Strategy #4

Students behave best when they believe you care. Before you punish, ask a student if s/he is all right.

What is:

You have some challenging students in your class. List three of them here by first name or initials:

_____ _____ _____

What have you done to try to improve their behaviors so far?

1. _____
2. _____
3. _____
4. _____
5. _____
6. _____

Draw a line through those things you have tried that only address the visible behavior, not the cause behind it.

Circle the things you have done that show you care about these students.

How many caring things have you tried? _____ Are you pleased with your number? Why or why not?

_____
_____
_____
_____
_____

What could be:

Imagine you are a teacher who is widely known by students as the most kind and supportive teacher in the school. Students trust you and know that you care. How would it feel to have that reputation?

_____

_____

_____

_____

_____

Imagine that your most challenging student is acting out in his/her most typically challenging way. Picture yourself going to that child, squatting down beside him/her, and saying, "Are you all right?" Wait for a response. What happens? What does the child say?

_____

_____

_____

_____

_____

What might change in the child's behavior as a result of showing you care?

_____

_____

_____

_____

Make it real:

Hint: When you want to ask a student if he or she is all right, be sure to ask in a private, quiet conversation with a sincere tone. Never ask with sarcasm, in front of peers, or without offering time for the child to find the courage or trust to share his/her truth.

Try this "Are you all right?" strategy as many times as possible in the next week with unhappy, disengaged, distracted, misbehaving, or bored students. Make a note of the child and his/her response. Notice if the behaviors improve. Keep this type of log:

Child's Name: _____

Upsetting Behavior: _____

Child's response to "Are you all right?": _____

Changes in behavior after expressing concern: _____

_____

_____

_____

Child's Name: _____

Upsetting Behavior: _____

Child's response to "Are you all right?": _____

Changes in behavior after expressing concern: _____

_____

_____

_____

Child's Name: _____

Upsetting Behavior: _____

Child's response to "Are you all right?": _____

Changes in behavior after expressing concern: _____

_____

_____

_____

Stay Near, Dear
Classroom Solution/Strategy #5

Students behave best when an adult is close by. Leave your comfort zone. Teach all around the room.

What is:

Draw a map of your classroom in the space below. Show students' desks, tables, your desk, and so forth. Draw a circle in the area(s) of the classroom you believe you tend to gravitate toward the most while teaching.

As you study your diagram, what areas do you notice that you tend to avoid while teaching?

_____

_____

_____

_____

Circle in a different color pen or marker the areas of the classroom where you feel you should spend more time if you truly desire proximity to your students while you teach. (Hint: Pay attention to where your challenging students sit.)

11

Invite a colleague, your principal, mentor, or team teaching partner to come and observe you during a lesson. Use a map of your classroom to have the observer mark an X where you are standing at 1-minute intervals of your teaching. Are you pleased with the proximity to your students, especially your troublesome students?

What could be:

Consider changes you could make in your classroom to have better proximity to your students.

♦ Could you rearrange the furniture in the classroom for better movement and access to the students? How?

_____

_____

_____

♦ Could you stand in different places during different aspects of your lesson? Explain.

_____

_____

_____

Redesign your classroom space and teaching habits for better movement around the room. In the space below, draw your new classroom map.

Make it real:

Invite that colleague, principal, or teaching partner for a return visit. Have the observer mark an X where you are in the classroom at 1-minute intervals. Does your new style/design allow for better proximity?

What do you notice about behavior problems in your class?

_____

_____

_____

_____

_____

Believe in Them!
Classroom Solution/Strategy #6

Students' behavior improves if they believe their teacher believes in them!

What is:

Do you believe in your students? Every single one of them? Are you thinking, "Yes … well … but …"? Write an honest answer to this question here:

_____

_____

_____

_____

_____

Have you ever given up on a student? How do you feel about having given up on him/her now that some time has passed?

_____

_____

_____

_____

It's easy to say, but hard to do! Believing in every single one of your students, that is.

What does a teacher who truly believes in his/her students *look like* during a class lesson?

_____ _____ _____

_____ _____ _____

_____ _____ _____

_____ _____ _____

What does a teacher who truly believes in his/her students *sound like* during a class lesson?

_____   _____   _____

_____   _____   _____

_____   _____   _____

How do the descriptions you have written above match with what an observer in your classroom would see and hear as you teach?

_____

_____

_____

_____

What could be:

Make a list of *phrases* that will convey to even the toughest student that you believe in him/her. (Ex: "That's it! I knew you knew that!" "Hey! That's the kind of great idea I expected from you!")

_____   _____

_____   _____

_____   _____

_____   _____

_____   _____

Make a list of *behaviors and body language* that would convey to even your toughest student that you believe in him/her. Share both lists with colleagues to compile a long and compelling list of phrases and behaviors. (Ex: Kneel down next to students to help them at their desks, smile warmly when they ask for help, look them in the eyes when you say you believe in them, etc.)

_____   _____

_____   _____

_____   _____

_____   _____

Make it real:

Now you have some tools—behaviors and words to show your students you believe in them. Use them often and wisely. Notice any behavior changes in your students. Write about three incidents where you showed faith in a student. Explain what you did and the results.

Student/Incident #1:

_____

_____

_____

_____

_____

_____

Student/Incident#2:

_____

_____

_____

_____

_____

_____

Student/Incident #3:

_____

_____

_____

_____

_____

_____

In a group of your colleagues, share your best "I believe in you" plans.

Meting Out the Seating:
Classroom Solution/Strategy #7

Your classroom seating arrangement affects behavior. Thoughtfully plan a variety of seating assignments.

What is:

Describe your current method for assigning seats in your classroom and explain it to a colleague.

_____

_____

_____

What is the *reason* for the way you currently assign seating?

_____

_____

_____

Is it a reason with good pedagogical theory to support it?

_____

Do you change the seating arrangement for your class during the semester, quarter, day? What reasons prompt you to change a seating assignment?

_____

_____

_____

Are some reasons for changing seating assignments better than others? Discuss this with a colleague.

What could be:

Read each of the following statements about seating assignments. Write **A** for Agree or **D** for Disagree and respond with your reason. Discuss your responses with several colleagues.

_____ Students should feel comfortable with where they are seated and with whom they are seated.

Why or why not? _____

_____ Let the students sit where they choose at first.

Why or why not? _____

_____ Assign seats on the first day and let the students get used to it.

Why or why not? _____

_____ Most students are very capable of sitting next to friends and not causing disturbances.

Why or why not? _____

_____ Friends should usually be separated. Students who do not get along should always be separated.

Why or why not? _____

_____ Cooperative group assignments or partner assignments are best if they are teacher assigned.

Why or why not? _____

_____ Once a seating chart/assignment has been developed that works in the class, do not change it.

Why or why not? _____

_____ There are times when the teacher should assign seating and times when students can decide.

Why or why not? _____

Make it real:

The authors shared several approaches for adjusting seating in the classroom. You may also want to do the following:

Give students a short survey about their seating assignment. You might be surprised at their responses. In your survey, ask questions such as:

- How do you feel about where you are sitting (front, back, middle, side, etc.)?
- Where would you prefer to sit? Why?
- Where else in the classroom would you like to be seated? Why?
- Is there anyone in class whom you believe it would be difficult to be seated near?

Use your observations and the student survey data to develop a new seating plan. Try it. Give the new plan some time. Note those seating assignments that are not working. Make changes if needed.

In advance of changing those seating assignments that are not working, plan what you will say to students about the change. Keep the reasons plausible and unrelated to behavior.

Notice the changes in behavior when you thoughtfully plan seating assignments and change them as needed. An effective seating arrangement in your classroom will have a positive impact on learning and behavior.

Happy Notes to Parents
Classroom Solution/Strategy #8

Informing parents of the GOOD things their children do can result in improved student behavior in the classroom!

What is:

Out of every 10 parent phone calls you make or notes you send to parents, how many are positive? _____ How many are about problems? _____

Is your ratio of positive communications at least double your negatives? _____

Can you improve your current ratio? What is your goal for positive to negative contacts? _____:_____

What could be:

What will parents believe about a teacher who takes time to share positive comments about their children?

_____

_____

_____

_____

_____

When you do need to share something negative about a student with his or her parents, how is it likely to be received if you have taken time in the past to send positive notes and establish a positive relationship?

_____

_____

_____

_____

_____

When sending positive notes home to parents, having multiple titles for various behaviors at the ready enables you to send a specific message home. A few starter ideas are listed below. Develop various possible titles for your "Happy Notes" below. Share these with two colleagues. You will generate even better ideas as a team.

+ "Student of the Day"
+ "Today's Star Student!"
+ "You'll Be So Proud of Your Child"
+ "Good News Note"

_____   _____   _____

_____   _____   _____

_____   _____   _____

To truly create something special that every child/parent will appreciate, consider these ideas and add your own to them:

+ Use colorful stationery and fun computer graphics.
+ Make the announcement of the student of the day a big event at the end of your class each day.
+ Your ideas here:

_____

_____

_____

_____

_____

_____

Make it real:

You will want to make a template of your daily note. Draw the draft design for your daily note/message to send home with at least one student each day in the space provided on the next page. Include student's name, date, reason for the award, your signature, and anything else you deem important.

Hint: Use word processing and computer graphics, not a hand-written format, in order to make it look professional and appealing.

Reminders!

- Don't leave anyone out! Over time, every child should receive at least one "Happy Note" from you.
- Develop a quick class list chart and put a check and/or date by each student's name every time s/he receives a Happy Note.
- Be sure to be fair and notice everyone's great behavior. For those challenging students, discretely, over time, give them more Happy Notes than others who may not need the constant positive messages.

Don't get stuck on one or two behaviors! Look at everything children do. What are the behaviors you will want to notice? Complete the list below with your own ideas.

- Offering a kind word to another student
- Paying attention during the assembly
- Following instructions the first time they are given
- Walking in line appropriately
- Staying seated for the entire activity
- Getting all materials out and ready for work
- Sharing a great idea to help the group
- Turning in homework _____ days in a row
- Being helpful to classmates

♦ Asking a great question
♦ Taking the lead in the group project
♦ Telling the truth about a situation

_____   _____

_____   _____

_____   _____

_____   _____

_____   _____

Their Own Notes to Parents: Classroom Solution/Strategy #9

It's always more effective for children to tell their parents that they misbehaved than it is for the teacher to tell the parents about the misbehavior.

What is:

What do you currently do when a student's misbehavior warrants telling his/her parents?

_____

_____

_____

_____

What pitfalls does your current plan have? Do parents ever begin to question you about whether the child truly did what you say s/he did? Write a brief summary of a time when telling a parent about a child's behavior got you caught up in defending yourself unnecessarily.

_____

_____

_____

_____

What could be:

What are the positives of having students write a note home or call parents themselves when they misbehave?

_____

_____

_____

What problems might you foresee with this strategy? If you have identified a potential problem, devise a strategy to solve it.

_____

_____

_____

_____

_____

Things to consider:

♦ Do you have all your parent/guardian phone numbers organized and ready? You can save a lot of time if you keep that database handy.

♦ Have a plan if a child does not return the note you sent to parents.

♦ Sometimes family dynamics make it unwise to send a note or make a phone call home. Teachers must first consider a child's safety and emotional health. If you feel that a child's safety is at stake, you may want to consider having him/her write the note to the principal or to the school counselor. Then you can discuss with these people how to best address the problem.

Make it real:

Many teachers use preprinted forms for students to write about misbehavior. These can be used to send home with a return signature requested. Writing what happened can help a child calm down and consider the facts of the matter more clearly than enduring a scolding or simply being ignored in detention or time out. Develop a form based on the example on the next page that you might use for students to complete when they misbehave. Share your form with a few colleagues and get some good ideas to add to yours.

Have several copies of your form ready next time parents need to know about misbehavior.

Name: _____ Date: _____

What happened? _____

_____

_____

_____

_____

(Write on the back if you need more space)

Where did this happen? _____

_____

When did this happen? (class, recess, lunch, bus, etc.) _____

_____

Next time I am in this situation, I will respond more appropriately. Here is what I'll do next time:

_____

_____

_____

The people I need to apologize to are: _____

_____

This is what I want to say to my parents/caretakers: _____

This is the truth about what happened and how I feel. _____

　　　　　　　　　　　　　　　　　　　　　　　　　Student signature

Comment from the teacher: _____

_____

Parents, please sign and return to school. Thank you for your continued support.

Teacher signature: _____

Parent/guardian signature: _____ Date: _____

Make Them Responsible:
Classroom Solution/Strategy #10

Students who are given authority and responsibility, within reason, in the classroom tend to demonstrate responsible behavior.

What is:

Consider the classroom responsibilities and duties you give students now. Circle the statement below that best describes you:

I give my students very little responsibility in my classroom, as I want to be in control.

I give my students some responsibility, but maybe I could give them a little more.

I have a plan for each of my students to have certain responsibilities in my classroom.

What could be:

What are three changes you could make in your classroom routine that would offer your students more responsibilities?

Hint: If you are having trouble coming up with ideas, ask a colleague to share ideas with you.

1. _____
2. _____
3. _____

Many teachers, at all grade levels, have classroom "jobs" for students. Sometimes, these jobs are assigned for a period of time, like a week or a month. Other times, the teacher assigns a responsibility to a particular student as he/she sees a need. For instance, one student may be responsible for collecting homework every day for a week. Another student may have the job, just for one day, of passing out papers to his classmates. One may be responsible for erasing the board. Another may be responsible for delivering something to the office. On the next page, list at least 10 jobs.

1. _____

2. _____

3. _____

4. _____

5. _____

6. _____

7. _____

8. _____

9. _____

10. _____

Make it real:

Set a Goal:

Give it a try! But first think about logistics. How will you assign and rotate jobs and responsibilities? Weekly? Daily? Random drawing? Rotation? Based on merit? Student choice?

Write a brief action plan telling how you will delegate certain authorities to your students. Will you assign jobs? What jobs will you assign? Will you allow the class to become more active in making certain classroom decisions? Are there some responsibilities you may want to share with your students? What are they, and how will you go about involving your students?

Action Plan:

_____

_____

_____

_____

_____

_____

_____

_____

_____

Stress Success, Not Duress: Classroom Solution/Strategy #11

Success truly does breed success. Notice student successes, stressing the positive things that they do. You will begin to see even more success!

What is:

If someone made a recording of your teaching during a 50-minute lesson, what number of positive remarks do you believe would be recorded? _____ How many negative, sarcastic, or critical remarks would be recorded? _____ Is your estimate for these two questions something you are pleased with? Why or why not?

_____

_____

_____

_____

_____

_____

The authors share the success of a teacher who was observed never making a critical or negative remark to her students. What comments do you often make to students that are positive?

_____ _____ _____

_____ _____ _____

_____ _____ _____

What comments might you make that students could construe as critical, sarcastic, or negative?

_____ _____ _____

_____ _____ _____

_____ _____ _____

What could be:

It is time to add to your "comment bank." For each of the categories below, make a list of positive comments you could begin using with your students tomorrow. Then share your lists with one or more colleagues and add their ideas to your list.

Comments about attention and participation in class:

_____

_____

_____

_____

_____

Comments about quality of homework:

_____

_____

_____

_____

_____

Comments about quality of class work:

_____

_____

_____

_____

_____

Comments about attitude in class:

_____

_____

_____

_____

_____

Comments about responsible actions you observe:

_____

_____

_____

_____

_____

Comments about effort:

_____

_____

_____

_____

_____

Comments about student behavior: Comments about improvement:

_____   _____

_____   _____

_____   _____

_____   _____

_____   _____

_____   _____

Other comments:

_____   _____

_____   _____

_____   _____

_____   _____

_____   _____

_____   _____

Is it difficult for you to be positive? What personal beliefs or attitudes might be affecting any negative comments you make?

_____

_____

_____

_____

Consider how it would feel to be the type of teacher described in this chapter. *You can be someone who is extremely positive, has students making outstanding progress, and takes great pride in students' accomplishments.* What do you need to do to become more like that type of teacher?

_____

_____

_____

_____

Make it real:

♦ Make an audio recording of yourself teaching a class. (This will be for your ears only.)

♦ Listen to it and count the number of positive comments you made to your students. Whatever the number, record yourself over the next several days, and try to increase your positive comments by at least 10% each day.

♦ Invite a colleague or principal in to observe and note the number of positive and negative statements you make. You'll enjoy great pride in your ability to teach and inspire children. Your colleagues will be inspired as well.

♦ What behaviors do you notice improving as you become more positive with students?

Enthusiasm Breeds Enthusiasm: Classroom Solution/Strategy #12

Enthusiastic teachers have fewer student behavior problems.

What is:

Rate your enthusiasm as a teacher:

Uninvolved and Bored	Disinterested but Trying to Smile	Happy and Satisfied	Exuberant and Joyful
1	2	3	4

Name an area of your life where you would definitely score a "4." (Fishing, traveling, being a friend to someone, being a parent, etc.)

_____

Would you be proud to share your teacher enthusiasm rating with a colleague? Why or why not?

_____

_____

How would you feel if your doctor, lawyer, financial analyst, tax accountant, or spouse held for you and your needs the same enthusiasm you hold for your students?

_____

_____

_____

Do your students deserve an enthusiastic teacher?

_____

_____

_____

Even if you are already an enthusiastic teacher, can you become even more so?

_____

_____

_____

What could be:

What comments or statements do students typically make about a teacher who is enthusiastic about teaching? List comments here:

_____   _____

_____   _____

_____   _____

_____   _____

_____   _____

Next to the student comments you just listed, place a check next to those that students might be saying about you now. Circle the comments you wish students said about you.

A picture of you, as a more enthusiastic teacher, is emerging. How do you like the picture you see?

_____

_____

Make it real:

List three adjectives that describe ENTHUSIASM in a teacher after each letter below.

E	Eager	_____	_____
N	Never unprepared	_____	_____
T	Tireless	_____	_____
H	_____	_____	_____
U	_____	_____	_____
S	_____	_____	_____
I	_____	_____	_____
A	_____	_____	_____
S	_____	_____	_____
M	_____	_____	_____

Select five characteristics that you intend to work on so that parents, students, and even coworkers will be more likely to use these when they describe you.

_____

_____

_____

_____

_____

Note the change in how you feel about yourself and how your students' behavior improves when you live, work, and teach with enthusiasm!

Pry for Why:
Classroom Solution/Strategy #13

Teachers who take time to find out the reason behind a child's behavior can better help that child improve the behavior.

What is:

How do you usually react when a child misbehaves? Do you:

a. Punish or scold the child, and forget about it?

b. Punish or scold the child, and then find out why he misbehaved?

c. Talk to the child before you decide on a punishment?

d. Talk to the child first, but always have a consistent punishment, regardless of the reason for the misbehavior?

Whether you chose a, b, c, or d, do you handle the situation privately or publicly?

What could be:

What do you feel you could improve on when dealing with student misbehavior? (Dealing with situations more privately, expressing more concern when dealing with misbehavior, delving deeper into why the misbehavior occurred, etc.)

_____

_____

_____

What belief or aspect of your discipline approach needs to change in order for you to reach that goal?

_____

_____

_____

Make it real:

Make a list of questions or statements to use with students who are misbehaving in order to find out *why* they are acting inappropriately. Work with a colleague to develop your list. Show your list to your school's counselor to gain tips and additional ideas for what to say and how to say it.

Example:

♦ "Sam, what's going on? I know this isn't who you really are."

♦ "Sally, I see you are upset. Why?"

♦ "Todd, you seem really angry about something. Let's talk. I'd like to help."

_____

_____

_____

_____

_____

_____

_____

Consider how you can add to the power of your carefully worded questions and/or statements to increase the chance of getting your students to open up and talk to you.

♦ How will you approach the child?

♦ What body language and facial expressions will you use?

♦ When will you try to ask the child about the "why"—how quickly during or after the behavior?

♦ What tone of voice will you want to use?

♦ What if you are still upset about the behavior yourself?

♦ How will you use proximity with the child? Sit beside him/her? Kneel in front?

As a general rule, wait until you are calm before dealing with the child, unless, of course, the situation warrants otherwise and others are in danger. Give the child time to calm down. Use good professional judgment and your caring intuition as a teacher.

Name one child whose behaviors are a challenge for you. Describe explicitly what you will do and say next time this child presents a difficult behavior.

_____

_____

_____

_____

_____

_____

_____

_____

After you have tried the above, write what happened. Are there things you could improve on the next time you deal with a similar situation?

_____

_____

_____

_____

_____

_____

_____

_____

_____

_____

_____

_____

_____

_____

_____

_____

A Laugh is Half:
Classroom Solution/Strategy #14

Teachers who make appropriate laughter and fun part of their daily classroom routine experience fewer behavior problems.

What is:

The authors listed 10 statements teachers made regarding the use of laughter in their classrooms. Read them again and place a "B" beside those that best describe what you BELIEVE about laughter in the classroom.

Now indicate with a "P" which of those 10 statements reflect what you PRACTICE in your classroom.

Is there a disconnect in your beliefs and practices? _____ If so, what is your reaction to that fact?

_____

_____

_____

What would someone who knows you and your teaching style say you have:

♦ Plenty of laughter

♦ Some laughter

♦ Not enough laughter

♦ No Laughter

What could be:

Bringing laughter into your classroom might feel uncomfortable at first if it is not part of your daily routine. What are some strategies that will help you begin to use more laughter in your classroom? A few suggestions are listed on the next page. Add your own ideas and then join two or more colleagues in completing a list of shared ideas to get you started.

Establish "Joke of the Day" and invite students to bring a joke they would like to share. Let them sign up with a number, draw a number at random, and so on.

Have a "Jokes" bulletin board. Invite students to bring comics, jokes, magazine/newspaper clippings of silly headlines, cartoons, and so on. You can also add your own jokes to this board. (Of course, you will have to approve what goes onto the bulletin board before it is placed there.)

Laugh at yourself! Share funny things that happen to you and allow students to do the same.

Purchase a joke book and allow students to take turns browsing and selecting a joke to share. Or share one joke from the book each day to start the class.

Incorporate humor and fun into your lessons and activities.

Now for your ideas:

_____

_____

_____

_____

Make it real:

From the previous list, decide where you will start. What strategy will you use, starting tomorrow, to introduce laughter and fun into your classroom? Describe what you will do here:

_____

_____

_____

_____

A few reminders:

Laughter at someone else's expense is never appropriate. Make this abundantly clear. The use of sarcasm is not a form of humor to be encouraged in a classroom. Many students do not understand sarcasm. Also, sarcasm is often an unkind way to use humor as a pretense for being hurtful.

What other guidelines might you want to consider if you ask students to share jokes and funny stories?

_____

_____

_____

_____

_____

_____

Student or Teaching Problem: Classroom Solution/Strategy #15

Teaching effectively and controlling your own behavior leads to fewer student behavior problems.

What is:

Children do behave differently in different classrooms. Name some teaching colleagues or teachers you had as a student who always seem/seemed to have fewer behavior problems than others.

_____ _____ _____

_____ _____ _____

What is it about those teachers that you believe might be contributing to their success with behavior management?

_____

_____

_____

Rate yourself on the aspects of quality teaching the authors list in this chapter.

1 = Lacking   2 = Satisfactory   3 = Good, but room to grow   4 = Excellent

My classroom procedures are evident	1	2	3	4
My classroom organization is evident	1	2	3	4
I have positive rapport with my students	1	2	3	4
I am visibly enthusiastic when I teach	1	2	3	4
I plan so there is no "down time" in class	1	2	3	4
I ensure success for each of my students	1	2	3	4
My lessons are well planned, relevant, and engaging	1	2	3	4

I treat each of my students with dignity	1	2	3	4
I do not allow my frustration to show or my "buttons" to be pushed by students	1	2	3	4

What do you notice about your ratings? Were you entirely honest with yourself? What surprised or pleased you about your ratings?

_____

_____

_____

_____

_____

What could be:

The authors suggest selecting one issue from the list above that is missing in your classroom and developing a plan for improvement. Make a plan. Begin by answering the following questions:

Which aspect of teaching from the authors' list will you select for improvement?

_____

_____

What parts of that issue are at least present in your teaching?

_____

_____

What do you need to do to start improving in this one aspect of your teaching?

Step 1. _____

Step 2. _____

Step 3. _____

When will you begin this new approach?

_____

On what particular students will your new approach have the most positive impact?

_____   _____   _____

_____   _____   _____

How will you know if it is working? What evidence or data can you gather? What will you see, hear, or experience if it is working?

_____

_____

_____

_____

_____

How long do you think it may take for your new approach to show an impact on the behaviors you want to change in your students?

_____

_____

Make it real:

The authors remind us that our reactions to students who push our buttons can exacerbate students' behaviors. What are some of your teaching "buttons"? If you do not know, ask your students. They do!

_____   _____   _____

_____   _____   _____

Strategy #17 goes into more detail about those buttons. Check it out!

Learn What to Overlook:
Classroom Solution/Strategy #16

Teachers who ignore or deflect most attention-seeking behaviors have better classroom control.

What is:

The authors suggest that many minor behaviors are overlooked by effective teachers. Consider this list. Which of these behaviors usually cause you to stop teaching? Circle them.

Tapping pencil	*Rolling eyes*	*Slumped in a seat*	*Book not open*
Doodling	*Daydreaming*	*Whispering*	*Sleeping*
Silly noises	*Giggling*	*Passing notes*	*Cell phone texting*
Reading a novel	*Unpleasant look*	*Slamming books*	*Not working at all*
Incorrect grammar	*Drawing*	*No eye contact*	*Bad language*
Gum chewing	*Mumbling*	*Defiant words*	*Refusal to answer*
Comment under breath	*Poking another student*		

Now draw a line through the behaviors above that you already ignore or could intentionally ignore.

What other behaviors typically cause you to stop teaching?

_____   _____   _____

_____   _____   _____

_____   _____   _____

_____   _____   _____

What could be:

What types of behaviors could you ignore? Underline those you cannot ignore. Add two other behaviors that you COULD ignore.

♦ Those that annoy me but do not interfere with my teaching

♦ Those that prevent me from teaching

♦ Those that prevent others in my class from learning

♦ Those that harm others in my class

♦ Those that annoy others but not me

♦ Those that are designed to get attention

♦ Those that humiliate others

♦ Those that prevent the misbehaving child from learning

♦ Those that take my students' attention away from me while I am teaching

♦ _____

♦ _____

Make it real:

From the list at the beginning of the "What is" section, select four specific behaviors that are challenging for you to ignore but might not be worth interrupting teaching and learning in order to address.

1. _____   2. _____

3. _____   4. _____

What, if anything, can you do or say for each of the above to deflect the behavior or redirect the student? For example, the authors suggest that if a student is not doing his/her work, the teacher can ask the student to do a favor for the teacher as soon as the work is complete in order to motivate the student to get busy.

Behavior #1 deflecting response: _____

_____

Behavior #2 deflecting response: _____

_____

Behavior #3 deflecting response: _____

_____

Behavior #4 deflecting response: _____

_____

Try it! Think of one student whose behavior annoys you, distracts you , or otherwise inhibits your teaching. Write his/her name here: _____

List two of the behaviors this child displays that you will now intentionally ignore.

    1. _____

    2. _____

What deflecting or redirecting responses or actions will you use to extinguish the behaviors?

    1. _____

    2. _____

    3. _____

    4. _____

If You Sweat, They Win:
Classroom Solution/Strategy #17

Teachers who remain in control of their actions and reactions with students deal with fewer behavior problems.

What is:

Everyone has buttons that can be pushed. There are certain phrases, behaviors, attitudes, words, and actions of others that infuriate, annoy, or provoke us. What are some of yours? List them here:

_____ _____ _____

_____ _____ _____

_____ _____ _____

Ask your closest friend, spouse, or partner for a few others to add to your list.

_____ _____ _____

_____ _____ _____

Ask a couple of your trusted teaching colleagues.

_____ _____ _____

_____ _____ _____

When someone at school (colleague, administrator, student, parent) pushes one of your buttons, how do you react? Consider your behavior honestly and list some of your typical reactions here:

When _____ happens, I _____

When _____ happens, I _____

When _____ happens, I _____

When _____ happens, I _____

Which of these reactions make you least proud?

_____

Why?

_____

Which reactions are you willing to eliminate?

_____   _____

_____   _____

What could be:

The authors suggest using practiced phrases or responding with a question when provoked. Think about ways you could react in order to maintain control when a button of yours is pushed. Prepare for those specific button-pushing situations now.

Imagine yourself in each of the "When _____ happens, I _____" statements on the previous page. Rewrite the second part of each sentence with a new reaction that would NOT result in showing frustration or a loss of control.

When _____ happens, I'll remain in control and (say or do)

_____

When _____ happens, I'll remain in control and (say or do)

_____

When _____ happens, I'll remain in control and (say or do)

_____

When _____ happens, I'll remain in control and (say or do)

_____

Make it real:

Select one of your buttons and keep a daily tally of how often it is getting pushed. For each tally, mark a "+" symbol if you did not react. Put a "−" when you do react. Can you reduce the minuses and increase your pluses over time?

Defuse the Bully:
Classroom Solution/Strategy #18

Teachers can defuse the perceived power of a bully by helping children understand the bully's nature.

What is:

Have you had students in your class who bullied others? Describe the bullying behaviors:

_____

_____

_____

_____

_____

What has been your typical response when observing bullying?

_____

What was the result of your intervention? Did the bullying stop?

_____

What could be:

In a class discussion, what points would you want to make about the following:

1. The nature of bullies. _____

   _____

   _____

2. The difference between tattling and reporting bullying behavior. _____

   _____

   _____

3. What choices victims of bullies have in handling the situation. _____

_____

_____

4. When witnessing a bullying incident, what actions might a student take?

_____

_____

_____

As a caring teacher, what can you say in a private conversation with a child who is bullying others? Remember that most children who act as bullies have been bullied themselves by friends or family.

_____

_____

_____

_____

Once a bullying incident has been reported to you, you must ACT! What are the options for you?

1. I can _____

2. I can _____

3. I can _____

4. I can _____

Make it real:

Name a child you have seen acting as a bully:

_____

Write two descriptions of this child. Write the first from the viewpoint of a teacher who does not have insight into the real cause of the bullying.

_____

_____

_____

Now write a description of this child from the viewpoint of a teacher with great insight into the real cause of this bully's behavior.

_____

_____

_____

Develop a plan for a discussion with your class regarding what to do about bullying.

♦ How will you begin the discussion or introduce the topic? _____

_____

_____

♦ How will you describe the three roles children play in bullying: bully, victim, witness?

A bully is _____

A victim is _____

A witness is _____

Develop a role-play script for your students to act out in your class. Practice the appropriate behavior for the victims and witnesses. Plan to act it out the wrong way first. Then, act it out the right way. Be sensitive about selecting someone to play the bully. It might be best for you to be the bully in your role play.

Role-play scenario title: _____

Here is what happens: _____

_____

_____

Here is what the *victim* did in the role play:
  Wrong thing: _____
  Right thing: _____

Here is what the *witness* did or said in the role play:
  Wrong thing: _____
  Right thing: _____

Hold Private Practice Sessions: Classroom Solution/Strategy #19

Privately discussing a student's challenging behavior and practicing the desired behavior can produce some amazing results.

What is:

When one of your students misbehaves, what do you usually do?

A. Address the behavior with the student while other students witness your reprimand.

B. Address the behavior with the student privately.

Use your own words and the content of Strategy 19 in the book to explain why choice A is not likely to be as effective as choice B. Imagine you are explaining the reason to someone who knows little about teaching or child psychology. Compare your answer with one or two colleagues.

_____

_____

_____

_____

What could be:

The authors suggest three parts to your "quiet" intervention:

1. Speak to the student privately about the problem, not in front of an audience, so as not to embarrass the child in front of others.

2. Speak as if you assume sincerely that the child has forgotten the correct way to behave or does not know what is expected.

3. Set up a private practice session with the student to practice the desired behavior. Explain that if the behavior occurs again, you will assume responsibility for not teaching the skill well and will schedule another practice session.

With three colleagues, role-play each of the scenarios below. Remember to speak sincerely and privately, assume responsibility for not teaching the skill well, and actually practice the skill.

Scenario 1: Hannah continues to talk to her neighbors, commenting with sarcasm or silly remarks as you are discussing a topic with the class. She tries to get a laugh or smirk from other students, especially the boys seated near her—and usually does. You have ignored the behavior and have not let her know it upsets you. However, her behavior continues and it is time to address it with her.

Scenario 2: Ben continues to turn in his papers without the standard name, date, and assignment name. You have explained this to your students several times. He is a bright boy and certainly knows what you would like him to do but he seems to be waiting for you to "notice." While this is easily ignored (you know his hand-writing and can identify which paper is his), it is time to make it clear that you expect him to follow procedures and comply with reasonable expectations.

Scenario 3: Elaine moves from learning station to learning station and assignment to assignment with the speed of a snail. She drags her feet and takes her time with great emphasis on frequent sighs of boredom, rolling of eyes, and overall lack of enthusiasm. It is clear she is waiting for you to say something. Other students stop and watch her move slowly about class during activity time and glance at you wondering if you are going to address this. Often they cannot get to the computer or start on the activity because they have to wait for Elaine. She seems to enjoy making others wait and is probably baiting you for a confrontation so she can deny she is doing anything wrong.

Make it real:

As you reflect on your own students, name one whose behavior is annoying, consistently inappropriate, and likely to be a need for attention.

What is the specific behavior you would like this child to change?

_____

Go through the three step process above and explicitly describe what you will say and do.

1. When and where will you speak to the student privately about the problem?

    _____

    _____

    _____

2. What will you say? Remember to speak as if you assume sincerely that the child does not know the correct way to behave or does not know what is expected.

    _____

    _____

    _____

3. When and where will you hold the practice session? What will you have your student do for practice?

    _____

    _____

    _____

Speak Awfully Softly: Classroom Solution/Strategy #20

A teacher's quiet, calm voice creates an environment conducive to good behavior.

What is:

Do you tend to get loud when speaking to your students?

_____

_____

_____

_____

When you get upset with a student, does your voice get louder or softer?

_____

_____

_____

_____

If you use a loud voice to get the attention of a group of students or respond to an angry student, do you find that the loud voice gets students' attention right away or do you repeat yourself, even with that loud voice?

_____

Do you believe that a quieter, calmer voice will get better attention and better responses from your students? Why or why not?

_____

_____

_____

_____

What could be:

Record yourself during a typical lesson.

As you listen to the recording, notice and respond to these questions:

When do you tend to raise your voice?

_____

_____

_____

_____

What happens to the volume of student voices in the classroom when your voice is raised?

_____

_____

_____

_____

During which parts of a lesson do you tend to use a quieter voice?

_____

_____

_____

_____

What happens to the volume of student voices in the classroom when your voice is quiet?

_____

_____

_____

_____

The authors also recommend leaning forward to convey importance in your message. Notice your body language as you talk to students. Rehearse this and watch for improvement in attention from your students.

Make it real:

Name a student who sometimes loses control and gets loud or confrontational.

_____

Make a plan for the next time that confrontation occurs.

+ Using a quiet, calm voice, say " _____ "
+ Lean toward the student and listen to his words, not his tone or volume.
+ Respond with a quiet, calm voice, saying, " _____ "
+ Never increase the volume of your voice.

What do you believe will happen to the student's volume, tone, and message as the conversation continues and you lean forward, listen, and respond quietly and calmly no matter how loud the student gets?

_____

_____

_____

Try it! Write what occurred with that student and share the results with a colleague next time you meet.

_____

_____

_____

_____

_____

_____

_____

_____

_____

_____

_____

_____

Teaching in Small Bites Makes Them Hungrier: Classroom Solution/Strategy #21

Breaking projects and large assignments into small, sequential steps creates success for everyone.

What is:

As a teacher, name two big, long-term tasks you complete each school year as part of your job (report cards, curriculum map, syllabus, work packets for a unit, etc.):

_____ and _____

Which is most like you in your approach to completing one of these two tasks?

A. I muscle through it right away and get it off my list in one marathon work session.

B. I develop a plan and timeline of intermediate goals or milestones and work through it piece by piece, completing it by the deadline.

C. I procrastinate, not getting started until the deadline is right in front of me. Then I sit down and get it done, but it is usually not my best work.

D. I really procrastinate and throw something together at the last minute, usually after the deadline. Then I turn it in and apologize profusely for not getting it done in time. I always have good reasons.

Which response would you prefer to have describe you? _____ How would this help your stress, work quality, and job satisfaction?

_____

_____

_____

_____

_____

Consider the long-term student projects you assign each year/semester.

List three:

_____

_____

_____

Which of the statements on the previous page (A-D) probably describes most of your students' approaches to these tasks? _____

Describe the explanation or lesson you use to introduce a project or long-term assignment. Use a similar narrative to the authors' examples of Teacher A and Teacher B.

_____

_____

_____

_____

_____

What do you notice about your explanation or introduction as you compare it to Teacher A/Teacher B examples in the text?

_____

_____

_____

_____

What could be:

Rethink this assignment or project. List the intermediate steps that you could assign in a step-by-step process to enable your students to successfully complete the project.

Step or Assignment 1: _____

Step or Assignment 2: _____

Step or Assignment 3: _____

Step or Assignment 4: _____

Step or Assignment 5: _____

Step or Assignment 6: _____

Make it real:

Rewrite the introduction or beginning explanation for one of your long-term assignments or projects, following the approach of Teacher B, not Teacher A. Describe how you will introduce the project and foster enthusiasm and confidence in the students for the task.

_____

_____

_____

_____

_____

_____

After the projects are completed, come back to this page and add notes or changes you will make the next time you give this assignment.

What did you notice about the rate of projects turned in on time? What about the quality of the projects compared to previous times you have assigned them? What about student motivation? What about their behavior during class time while working on their projects?

_____

_____

_____

_____

_____

_____

_____

_____

Saving "Gotcha" for Behaving: Classroom Solution/Strategy #22

Great teachers always notice when students are doing things right, and they praise them for these behaviors.

What is:

Think about your teaching. Describe some "gotcha" comments you have made about students' behavior.

Behavior: _____

Gotcha comment: _____

Behavior: _____

Gotcha comment: _____

Behavior: _____

Gotcha comment: _____

Behavior: _____

Gotcha comment: _____

Did the four gotcha comments you listed refer to negative or positive behaviors?

_____

The authors remind us that great teachers make no negative gotcha comments. They save their gotcha comments for appropriate student behavior. They suggest talking to a student privately if a negative behavior cannot be ignored. How close are you to this goal as a teacher? On the next page, check the response box that best matches your current teaching behavior.

☐ I often comment on the negative things my students do.

☐ I comment on some positives but usually talk more to those students who are misbehaving.

☐ I comment on both positive and negative behaviors about equally.

☐ I make mostly positive comments, but certain behaviors really irritate me and I tend to comment on those when they occur.

☐ I am an example of the effective teacher the authors mention in Strategy 22.

What could be:

Reread the four examples of a teacher using gotcha statements for misbehaving students. Consider what the teacher could have/should have said instead.

Instead of, "Well, how could you know? You haven't been paying attention," the teacher should have/could have ...

_____

_____

Instead of, "Did I say to talk while completing your worksheet?" the teacher should have/could have ...

_____

_____

Instead of choosing to single out the one student who had not completed his assignment and chastising him in front of the class, the teacher should have/could have ...

_____

_____

Instead of, "Where were you when we discussed this earlier?" the teacher should have/could have ...

_____

_____

Make it real:

Select in advance two lessons you will be teaching in the next few days. Monitor yourself making only positive statements about what students are doing well and ignoring (or dealing privately with) those behaviors that are contrary to what you expect. Take time after each lesson to reflect on what you are proud of or pleased with in your commentary and what you will aim to improve next time.

<table>
<tr><td>Lesson #1</td><td>Lesson #2</td></tr>
</table>

I'm proud of saying _____

_____

_____

_____

I was able to ignore _____

_____

_____

Next time I will improve _____

_____

_____

_____

I'm proud of saying _____

_____

_____

_____

I was able to ignore _____

_____

_____

Next time I will improve _____

_____

_____

_____

Find the Gleaming and Redeeming: Classroom Solution/Strategy #23

Finding what is gleaming and redeeming in your students makes them want to be even more so!

What is:

Circle the rating that best describes you as a teacher and person.

1 = Never   2 = Once in awhile   3 = Usually   4 = Often

I tell my colleagues about my students' successes more than failures.	1	2	3	4
I talk about my students to others in positive terms.	1	2	3	4
I compliment my students each day.	1	2	3	4
My students know I value them for who they are.	1	2	3	4
When I talk to students, I make more positive than critical remarks.	1	2	3	4
When I get together with friends, I speak mostly of positive experiences.	1	2	3	4

What changes could you make in order to become more positive with your students?

_____

_____

The authors say, "Life is what we focus on! And so it is in the classroom." Write three examples of what your classroom environment/culture/tone is like as a result of what you focus on when teaching.

1. My focus on _____ creates _____.

2. My focus on _____ creates _____.

3. My focus on _____ creates _____.

What could be:

List one area/task where you could better show appreciation to your students (homework completion, helpfulness, eagerness to learn, etc.).

_____

_____

_____

_____

With my students I will focus on the positive ways they ...

_____

_____

_____

Make it real:

List 10 of your students in order of most to least challenging. Write a comment for each that states what you value and appreciate about them. Use these with each of the students during the next week. Make these appreciative remarks often and watch students' behavior improve.

Name: Comment:

1. _____   _____

2. _____   _____

3. _____   _____

4. _____   _____

5. _____   _____

6. _____   _____

7. _____   _____
   _____   _____

8. _____   _____
   _____   _____

9. _____   _____
   _____   _____

10. _____   _____
    _____   _____

Join the Ranks of Thanks: Classroom Solution/Strategy #24

Praising and thanking students can motivate them and enhance good behavior.

What is:

The authors tell us that praise is a "valuable gift." List three instances where you have received praise recently.

1. _____

2. _____

3. _____

How did this praise make you feel? _____

_____

_____

_____

_____

Now list three student behaviors you tend to praise. Write what you typically say.

Situation: _____

I say, _____

Situation: _____

I say, _____

Situation: _____

I say, _____

What could be:

The authors give several examples of excellent teachers' use of "thank you" in classrooms. Place a check next to all below for which you thank your students.

- ☐ Entering class quietly
- ☐ Remembering to do homework
- ☐ Neatly written class notes
- ☐ Getting to work on an assignment very quickly
- ☐ Staying in one's seat during class
- ☐ Excellent piece of writing/story
- ☐ Closing the door
- ☐ Working well in a group
- ☐ Cleaning around desks before the bell
- ☐ Helping another student with class work
- ☐ Other

Make it Real:

List a few behaviors you will begin praising, not including, of course, those behaviors you already do praise.

_____   _____

_____   _____

_____   _____

_____   _____

_____   _____

You can create a "Thank You!" culture in your classroom. Students will follow your example.

Humiliation Breeds Retaliation: Classroom Solution/Strategy #25

Attempting to manage behavior by humiliating students causes resentment and often leads to retaliation.

What is:

The authors point out that most people have memories of being humiliated by a teacher. Reflect on your experiences as a student. Recall one time you were humiliated or saw a teacher humiliate another child. Write the story summary here and share it with one or two colleagues.

_____

_____

_____

_____

_____

Do you or your colleagues recall any retaliatory efforts made to "get even" with that teacher? Describe or discuss.

_____

_____

_____

_____

During your reflection of personal experiences, were you reminded of any time when you have used humiliation to get a student to stop misbehaving? If so, what might have been a more professional approach?

_____

_____

_____

_____

What could be:

Humiliation of a child can take many forms. Some are listed below. In each blank, list an alternative comment or response that would address the situation without humiliating the child.

Calling attention to a child's poor grades or lack of knowledge in front of the class

_____

Confronting a belligerent child, staring him/her down, backing him/her into a corner

_____

Standing over a child at his desk and shaming him about the quality of his work in front of others

_____

Mocking a child who raised his hand to ask a question about something you just explained thoroughly

_____

Make it real:

Why do you think teachers resort to humiliation as a form of behavior management? Discuss with two partners and come to some conclusions. Write them here.

Reasons:

1. _____

2. _____

3. _____

Have you ever resorted to using humiliation with students? Explain.

_____

_____

_____

Tell how you could have handled the aforementioned situation without humiliating the child.

_____

_____

_____

If you have used humiliation as a means to correct behavior in the past, is there anything you can now do or say to repair the teacher-student relationships that have been damaged? Explain.

_____

_____

_____

_____

_____

Beware the 90/10 Rule:
Classroom Solution/Strategy #26

Effective teachers rarely send students to the office. When they do, however, these referrals are taken seriously by the administration.

What is:

In the past 5 days of teaching, how many students have you sent to the office?
_____

In the past 5 weeks, how many students have you sent to the office? _____

Rate yourself by circling the statements below that best describe you.

- *I rarely send any child to the office.*
- *I send those same few problem students when they act up.*
- *I send many students to the office. I don't have time to deal with them.*

Compared to my colleagues I …

- *Send more students to the office than most teachers in my school*
- *Send about the same number of children to the office as others*
- *Send fewer students than most teachers in my school*

Why might sending students again and again to the office for a variety of reasons be an ineffective practice?

_____

_____

What is your purpose for sending children to the office? What do you expect to have happen there?

_____

_____

What message do you think it sends to students when teachers often send them to the office for minor infractions?

_____

_____

_____

The authors describe some effective teacher behaviors that prevent the need for office referrals. Circle those that could use some improvement in your own classroom.

- ♦ *Good classroom management*
- ♦ *Treat all students with dignity*
- ♦ *Teach from bell to bell*
- ♦ *Plan engaging lessons*
- ♦ *Address potential problems early*

What could be:

Consider your school's behavior expectations and consequences. What are the specific reasons that school rules or school board policy *require* a teacher to help a child "send himself" to the office? Look in your school's student handbook if you are not sure.

1. _____

2. _____

3. _____

4. _____

What is the powerful difference between telling your students "I'm sending you to the office for _____" and "Because you _____, you have sent yourself to the office"?

_____

_____

_____

_____

What behaviors occur in your classroom that cause you to send children to the office? What is an alternative response to those behaviors that could replace an office referral?

Behavior #1: _____ Alternative: _____

Behavior #2: _____ Alternative: _____

Behavior #3: _____ Alternative: _____

Behavior #4: _____ Alternative: _____

Behavior #5: _____ Alternative: _____

Did you list your own anger and frustration as reasons you send children to the office? Is this a valid reason to send them? _____ Why or why not?

_____

_____

Make it real:

What will you need to do differently when you (1) manage most behaviors yourself, (2) maintain your cool and control, and (3) stop referring students to the office for minor infractions? What will you need to tell your students? Who can help you with ideas, strategies, and support?

_____

_____

_____

_____

Plan your "speech" to your students about behavior in the style suggested in the book. Start with, *"I don't send anyone to the office for misbehavior."* Then what will you say?

_____

_____

_____

_____

We Care About Those Who Care About Us: Classroom Solution/Strategy #27

Students respond positively when they know their teachers care.

What is:

Teachers care about their students. But do they all say it explicitly? Do you?

Consider the ways you show and tell your students you care about them. List them here.

_____   _____

_____   _____

_____   _____

_____   _____

Some of the ways we show we care are not obvious to our students. On your list above, mark an "E" beside the ways you show and say you care that are "explicit" and clear to students. Mark an "I" for "implied" beside the ways you show you care that students might not realize. Is your caring more explicit or implied toward your students? _____

What could be:

Use the same "E" and "I" codes for these additional ways teachers often show they care.

_____ Staying up late to get all the tests scored so students get them back quickly.

_____ Talking to a student who did not do well on a test, saying, "I am concerned about your score because I care about you. What happened on the test?"

_____ Putting your hand on a child's shoulder as he's beginning to argue with another student about who is first in line and saying, "Hey, Sam, wait a minute. What's going on?"

_____ Saying to the boys arguing about lining up, "I care about you both and I'm upset to see you arguing. How can we show respect and caring and decide what to do here?"

_____ Attending the basketball game because three of your students are on the team.

_____ The day after the basketball game, saying to the three students, "I am so glad I went to the game and saw you play! You made a great rebound in the third quarter! I was really proud of your defense, too!"

The authors point out that the best time to say you care is at the moment a child is acting out. Write what the teacher should do or say to show caring in each of the following situations:

Cesar is sitting at the assembly poking the back of the girl sitting in front of him. He has a big smile on his face and looks at his buddy beside him as he is poking her.

_____

_____

Maria is standing with her hands on her hips at the computer station in the library loudly telling a boy seated there, "It's my turn now and you have to get off the computer!"

_____

_____

Adam just tripped over someone's foot in class. You see that it was accidental. However, Adam is turning to the child whose foot caused the trip with a stormy expression and with his fist raised.

_____

_____

Allison got her English research paper back with a grade of C–. She's upset. She slams her book shut, crosses her arms over her chest and says loudly to herself, "I'm sick of this!"

_____

_____

Make it real:

Now it is your turn. Describe briefly three behaviors you have addressed with one or more of your students recently. Then, write what you will do/say at the moment this happens again to show explicitly that you care about this child. Get input from a partner to be sure it is a skillfully designed response. Rehearse it so you are ready to use it!

Behavior 1: _____

_____

Explicit "I care" response: _____

_____

Behavior 2: _____

_____

Explicit "I care" response: _____

_____

Behavior 3: _____

_____

Explicit "I care" response: _____

_____

Be sure to plan what you will say when or if a child rebuffs your caring response at the moment of misbehavior. Do not be shocked or disappointed. Keep cool and be ready to continue to show how much you care. I might say,

_____

_____

_____

_____

_____

As Nice, Polite, and Motivated as You?: Classroom Solution/Strategy #28

Teachers who model positive attitudes and actions usually see them reflected in students' behaviors.

What is:

Assess yourself honestly on these factors as suggested by the authors:

Give yourself 4 for *Yes, Always*; 3 for *Usually and Often*; 2 for *Sometimes*; and 1 point for *No*.

1. Do I smile most of the time in the presence of my students? _____

2. Am I consciously nice to all of my students on a daily basis? _____

3. Do I take extra care to model courtesy in all situations? _____

4. Do I convey enthusiasm and motivation as I teach? _____

5. Do I reprimand my students in a dignified, calm, controlled way? _____

6. Am I respectful toward students at all times? _____

7. Would all my students likely describe me as a happy person? _____

8. Does every one of my students know for sure that I like him/her? _____

Total Score: _____

Score Analysis:

28-32 Good for you! You exemplify this strategy all the time!

20-28 You are doing well in this aspect of your teaching and there are a few behaviors to improve.

12-20 You demonstrate positive, polite, and motivated teaching some of the time and need to do it more consistently and with each of your students.

8-12 This is an important strategy to develop in yourself. Polite, kind, motivated teaching every day with every child should become a priority in your professional development.

Consider what type of person your students see when they are with you. Do you want them to mirror you in their behavior? Why or why not?

_____

_____

What could be:

Circle three behaviors that you feel you could improve upon:

Always smiling   *Always nice*   *Always courteous*   *Always enthusiastic*

Always motivated   *Always calm*   *Always dignified*   *Always respectful*

Always happy   *Always showing others I truly like them*

Make it real:

You have just identified three aspects of your behavior you could improve upon in order to be a better model for your students. For each of the three descriptors you circled above, list two specific actions you will take toward improving or increasing your consistency in demonstrating those model behaviors.

Descriptor #1: Always _____

I will improve by:

    1. _____

    2. _____

Descriptor #2: Always _____

I will improve by:

    1. _____

    2. _____

Descriptor #3: Always _____

I will improve by:

    1. _____

    2. _____

Unmask the Mask:
Classroom Solution/Strategy #29

Great teachers always search for the reasons behind a child's misbehavior.

What is:

Children do behave in certain ways for certain reasons … good or bad. List some events or experiences in the categories below that might occur in a child's life to cause misbehavior:

Home/Family/Environment

_____ _____

_____ _____

_____ _____

Previous School/Class/Teachers

_____ _____

_____ _____

_____ _____

Organic/Physical/Health/
Birth/Medical

_____ _____

_____ _____

_____ _____

Social Experiences
(friends, peers)

_____ _____

_____ _____

_____ _____

Compare your list with colleagues.

What could be:

As you consider this list of misbehaviors often seen in children, think of the misbehavior as "The Mask" and the reason for the behavior as "What's Behind the Mask." For each behavior, write two possible reasons behind the mask that might explain the behavior. An example is completed for you.

81

The Face on the Mask	Behind the Mask
Matt never pays attention in class.	1. Matt is allowed to play video games until he falls asleep each night, usually 1 a.m. 2. Matt's parents fight constantly and he is worried.
Erika glowers at everyone every day, she wears only black, and she seems angry all the time.	1. _____ _____ 2. _____ _____
Tony is in fights with classmates constantly. He's so angry and he recoils any time someone tries to touch him or get close to him.	1. _____ _____ 2. _____ _____

Make it real:

Choose three students in your class who present constant and difficult behavior challenges. Describe what you know about their "behind the mask" experiences that probably contribute to these behaviors.

Name of Student: _____

   Behind the Mask Experiences:

   _____

   _____

   _____

Name of Student: _____

   Behind the Mask Experiences:

   _____

   _____

   _____

Name of Student: _____

Behind the Mask Experiences:

_____

_____

_____

What will you do differently as a result of knowing what is behind the mask for your most challenging students?

_____

_____

_____

_____

If you truly have no idea what "behind the mask" experiences a child has had, how can you find out?

_____

_____

_____

_____

Explain how you can apply the third step the authors describe: *"Never take a child's behavior personally."*

_____

_____

_____

_____

Don't Let the Mood Brood: Classroom Solution/Strategy #30

The very best teachers know how to defuse the angry moods of students.

What is:

Make a list of 10 ways a child shows a teacher s/he's in a bad mood. Remember, there are words, actions, and body language that tell the story. If you cannot think of 10, find a colleague to help you complete the list. Examples: slams books on desk, refuses to answer simple greeting, and so on. (Only fill in the first column for now.)

To show they are in a bad mood, students …	My usual response to this is …	I, D, or C?
1.	*	
2.	*	
3.	*	
4.	*	
5.	*	
6.	*	
7.	*	
8.	*	
9.	*	
10.	*	

*Once you've completed your list, write what your reaction is when this behavior occurs in your class.

Now, in the third column at the far right, write "I" if your response resembles Mrs. IgnoreYa, write "D" if your response is like Mrs. DontYaDare, and write "C" if your response is like Mrs. ICare.

How many Is? _____ How many Ds? _____ How many Cs? _____

What could you do to become even more like Mrs. ICare?

_____

_____

_____

What could be:

For each of the examples of a student's moody behavior below, write a description of a response an excellent teacher might use to divert or change the mood.

You say, "Good morning" to Brittany as she enters your class and her eyes immediately stare into yours with daggers in them. Her lips are set firm and she is frowning. She quickly shifts her body away from you and brushes past you to her seat, throwing her books on the floor.

Your response:

_____

_____

_____

David comes in with eyes averted, head down trying to avoid eye contact. You think you detect some tears forming. He shrugs up his jacket and tries to duck as much of his head down into the coat as he can. You go over and reach out to touch his arm. He jerks away angrily.

Your response:

_____

_____

_____

Gina responds to your greeting with a flip of her hair, a toss of her chin. As she sits, she looks at you, rolling her eyes and curling her lip in a sneer as if you are the most disgusting creature on the planet.

Your response:

_____

_____

_____

Make it real:

Now write a description of three moods you have seen students bring into your class. Describe how those moods present themselves below. Next, complete the statements below the description.

Moody Behavior #1

_____

_____

_____

Instead of ignoring *or negatively* confronting *this student and the behavior, I will:*

_____

_____

Moody Behavior #2

_____

_____

_____

Instead of ignoring *or negatively* confronting *this student and the behavior, I will:*

_____

_____

Moody Behavior #3

_____

_____

_____

Instead of ignoring *or negatively* confronting *this student and the behavior, I will:*

_____

_____

Who's the Most Positive?: Classroom Solution/Strategy #31

Students respond positively to the most positive teachers.

What is:

The authors ask you to name the most positive person in your school. Write that person's name here: _____

Name three other people who came to mind as you considered your most positive colleagues.

_____   _____   _____

Are *you* one of the names of the four listed above? _____

If not, are you close to being on the list or far from it? _____

_____

_____

Imagine you are working in your room before school and one of those very positive people from your list stops by. How do you feel when you look up and see that person at your door?

_____

_____

_____

Now imagine you pop into several other teachers' rooms one morning to ask a question or just to say hello. How do you want them to feel about seeing you at their door?

_____

_____

_____

What could be:

List the evidence. What do you observe from those positive people that caused you to put them on your list? Name six things.

_____   _____

_____   _____

_____   _____

What do you believe students would say about a teacher whom they believe is the *most* positive teacher they have ever had? What would they say this teacher says, does, and believes? List six things.

1. _____

2. _____

3. _____

4. _____

5. _____

6. _____

Imagine that your students are interviewed by a neutral person about having you for their teacher. What are six things they will probably say about you?

1. _____

2. _____

3. _____

4. _____

5. _____

6. _____

Do these two lists match? _____ Explain. _____

_____

_____

_____

Make it real:

What would be the *benefits to you* if you were considered by *colleagues* to be the most positive person in the school? List three:

1. _____
2. _____
3. _____

What would be the *benefits to you* if you were considered by *students* to be the most positive teacher in the school? List three:

1. _____
2. _____
3. _____

What would be the *benefits to your students* if their teacher (you) were truly the most positive teacher in the school? List six benefits.

1. _____
2. _____
3. _____
4. _____
5. _____
6. _____

Now consider what you can do or say differently or more often in order to develop the reputation as the most positive teacher in the school in the eyes of your colleagues. List four things.

1. _____
2. _____
3. _____
4. _____

What about your students? What are eight things you will start doing or saying so your students come to view *you* as the most positive teacher they have ever had?

1. _____

2. _____

3. _____

4. _____

5. _____

6. _____

7. _____

8. _____

Become Interested in Their Interests: Classroom Solution/Strategy #32

The most effective teachers always take time to learn about the interests of their students.

What is:

Name 10 of your students. Beside each name, write his/her specific interests.

	Name:	*Interests:*
1.	_____	_____
2.	_____	_____
3.	_____	_____
4.	_____	_____
5.	_____	_____
6.	_____	_____
7.	_____	_____
8.	_____	_____
9.	_____	_____
10.	_____	_____

Out of 10 students, for how many could you list specific interests? ____ out of 10.

8-10 out of 10 = GREAT!

5-8 out of 10 = Pretty Good! There is room to improve but you know many of your students' interests.

3-5 out of 10 = You have invested in learning about a few of your students. Now get to know them all.

0-3 out of 10 = This is a good strategy for you to develop with a great likelihood that you will notice improvement in relationships with and behaviors of your students.

What could be:

List specific interests that students you teach have in each category.

Popular Books	*Popular Television Shows*	*Popular Movies/ Videos*	*Popular Video Games*
_____	_____	_____	_____
_____	_____	_____	_____
_____	_____	_____	_____
_____	_____	_____	_____

Popular Sports	*Popular Music/ Musicians*	*Popular Hobbies*	*Popular Foods*
_____	_____	_____	_____
_____	_____	_____	_____
_____	_____	_____	_____
_____	_____	_____	_____

Popular Vehicles	*Popular Places to Eat*	*Places They Hang Out*	*After-School Activities*
_____	_____	_____	_____
_____	_____	_____	_____
_____	_____	_____	_____
_____	_____	_____	_____

How did you do? Could you name specific high-interest items for your students? Why is this important to know as a teacher?

_____

_____

_____

_____

_____

The authors suggest four ways to get to know the interests of your students. Their ideas are listed below. Rank their suggestions from 1-4 for their value to *you* in getting to know each of your students. Number 1 would be the best way for *you* to go about learning and becoming involved in what interests your students.

_____   Hold discussions that allow students to share their interests with you.

_____   Ask your students to complete an interest inventory.

_____   Observe and listen to your students closely.

_____   Attend after-school activities.

Now list three other ways you could get to know your students' interests. Here is one to get you started:

1. Invite a small group of students (three or four each time) to eat lunch with you each week. Use the lunch conversation to learn about their individual interests, hobbies, dreams, goals, and personalities.

     _____

2. _____

     _____

3. _____

     _____

4. _____

     _____

Make it real:

What is your plan? How will you pursue learning about each of your students' personal interests, passions, hobbies, and personalities?

I will:

_____

_____

_____

_____

_____

A Favor as a Lifesaver:
Classroom Solution/Strategy #33

Smart teachers often use "favors" as opportunities to give praise and to give students opportunities to cool down or refocus.

What is:

What kinds of jobs, errands, and other favors do you currently invite students to do for you? List them.

_____   _____   _____

_____   _____   _____

_____   _____   _____

_____   _____   _____

Circle the real reasons from the list below that you ask students to do favors for you.

To help me

To get them out of the room for a break

To have a reason to praise them

To help them feel good about themselves

To teach responsibility

To increase self-worth

To demonstrate trust or confidence in them

To save me time/effort

To distract a mood

To help them expend some energy

To keep them busy when finished with work

To show favoritism

To give me a break from a student

To stop a brewing argument between two students

Other: _____   _____

_____   _____

_____   _____

What could be:

How could you incorporate or adapt the "empty envelope" idea for your classroom?

Describe your plan here: _____

_____

_____

Work with your colleagues for a few minutes to generate a list of errands or favors you could ask students to do for you. Consider two categories below.

In the Classroom	*Away From the Classroom*
ex. Sharpen all my pencils	Get my mail from my school mailbox

Make it real:

Asking students to do favors for you can help your classroom behavior improve. Consider your students and the reasons they might benefit from doing favors or running errands for you.

Names of my students who need to feel important and valued:

_____ _____

_____ _____

Names of my students whom I need to praise more often:

_____ _____

_____ _____

_____ _____

Names of my students who have a hard time getting to work or completing tasks (use the "run an errand after you complete that work" strategy):

_____   _____

_____   _____

_____   _____

Names of my students who might need a "cooling off" opportunity to leave the room once in awhile:

_____   _____

_____   _____

_____   _____

Names of my students who have a need to organize, clean, put away, and make things orderly:

_____   _____

_____   _____

_____   _____

Take time to match a set of favors to each group of students. Then, enjoy watching their behavior improve.

Admit Your Mistakes:
Classroom Solution/Strategy #34

Admitting mistakes and using them as teachable moments and/or to reveal our humanness benefits students.

What is:

Which teacher in the text is most like you, Mrs. Right or Mrs. I. M. Human?

_____

Why? _____

Complete these statements (without looking back in the text if you can).

There is no _____ teacher.

The best teachers readily admit their _____.

Your mistakes and how you respond to them in class can allow you to become a positive _____ _____ (two words) for your students.

When a teacher never admits a mistake, students learn _____.

When a teacher admits a mistake, students learn _____.

What could be:

Are there circumstances when you make intentional mistakes for students to "catch"? If so, how could you do that and make your intent clear? Describe an example.

_____

_____

_____

_____

Think of three examples of unintentional mistakes you have made while teaching. Write a few sentences to describe how Mrs. I. M. Human would have responded or reacted in these two situations.

Mistake #1: _____

Mrs. I. M. Human's excellent response: _____

_____

_____

Mistake #2: _____

Mrs. I. M. Human's excellent response: _____

Mistake #3: _____

Mrs. I. M. Human's excellent response: _____

Make it real:

Admitting mistakes to your students teaches them that mature people admit mistakes, correct them, and learn from them without needing to defend, deny, blame, or otherwise avoid the error.

Consider other professional situations where admitting a mistake might do more good than putting energy into not admitting it. With a partner, plan an appropriate response to the following scenarios:

A parent comes to show you that you have incorrectly calculated his child's math exam score, and therefore the grade should be higher. You did miscalculate.

_____

_____

Your principal comes to tell you that he noticed you were not at your duty station this morning and there was a fight. The truth is, you got to work late and did not go to your duty station.

_____

_____

_____

At a parent conference, a parent refers to his child's IEP (Individualized Education Plan) and reminds you that you are supposed to allow extra time for tests. He says that his son reports that you are not doing this. The truth is that you did not know this was in his IEP, but you should have.

_____

_____

_____

The assistant principal stopped by to informally observe your class last week. Now she is back to speak with you about the lesson you taught. She says it was clear that you were not prepared and that you seemed to be pulling the lesson together on the spot. She is right.

_____

_____

_____

Seeing Eye to Eye:
Classroom Solution/Strategy #35

Positive eye contact shows that you value a student. Misbehaviors occur more when eye contact is absent.

What is:

The authors suggest that for one day you focus on making direct eye contact with each student. Do this or imagine yourself doing this. How does it feel (or how do you think it would feel)?

Fine, I'm good at making eye contact with everyone	*Less than comfortable but I do it most of the time*	*Uncomfortable except for a few of my students*	*Very uncomfortable*

Discuss the differences between the types of eye contact described in the text. Work with a partner to develop a definition for each.

Positive eye contact: _____

_____

_____

What does this type of eye contact teach students? _____

_____

_____

Serious eye contact: _____

_____

_____

What does this type of eye contact teach students? _____

_____

_____

Negative eye contact: _____

_____

_____

What does this type of eye contact teach students? _____

_____

_____

What type of eye contact do you usually use with students?

Positive eye contact   *Serious eye contact*   *Negative eye contact*   *No eye contact*

When you have used negative versus serious eye contact, was the typical student response what you hoped for? Did it eliminate the behavior? Why or why not?

_____

_____

_____

What could be:

If you make positive eye contact with each of your students every day, what results will probably occur for you and your students?

Relationships with students: _____

_____

Students' eye contact skills: _____

Behavior problems: _____

_____

When are the best times to use positive eye contact with your students? List them here in discussion with a partner:

Example: When the students enter my class _____

_____

_____

Make it real:

Make a plan. Describe three new practices in your classroom that will increase your positive eye contact with students.

1. _____

   _____

   _____

2. _____

   _____

   _____

3. _____

   _____

   _____

Complete this statement.

I will not use negative eye contact when students misbehave. Instead, I will respond by:

_____

_____

_____

_____

Bell-to-Bell Teaching: Classroom Solution/Strategy #36

When you teach from bell to bell, keeping your students engaged, behavior problems dissipate.

What is:

What is your typical response to a student who tells you that s/he has finished with the work and there is time remaining in the lesson period?

A. I have another activity planned related to the topic, and another after that for those who finish.

B. I have books and magazines, word find puzzles, and fun activities available for students to do.

C. I tell them to go ahead and read their library books, do other homework, or read the next chapter.

D. I let them draw, talk to others who are finished, or do whatever they like as long as they are quiet.

The authors suggest planning lessons that are student-oriented. What does that mean to you? Check with two other colleagues. Come up with a definition.

A student-oriented lesson _____

_____

To what degree are your lessons student-oriented?

Always   Usually   Sometimes   Rarely

For what portion of your lessons do you usually do the talking?

| *Almost the entire period* | *Most of the period* | *Some of the lesson period* | *Students do most of the talking* |

How often do you put students in groups to work together cooperatively?

Always   Usually   Sometimes   Rarely

Within a 50-minute lesson, how many changes in activity, grouping, or skills do you plan?

*We work for an entire   Half the lesson is   Three or four shorter
 period on one thing   one activity, half another   activities within one period*

What could be:

Based on your answers in the previous section, what areas are already strong aspects of your lesson planning?

_____

_____

_____

_____

_____

_____

What areas offer you room for improvement and development as a teacher?

_____

_____

_____

_____

_____

_____

What are some other teaching/planning skills that help a teacher teach from bell to bell?

1. _____

2. _____

3. _____

Make it real:

Describe two actual lessons you plan to teach in the near future. Write your objectives for the lesson using, "The students will _____."

Lesson #1. Describe briefly:

_____

_____

Rephrase in student behavior: *The students will* _____

Lesson #2. Describe briefly:

_____

_____

Rephrase in student behavior: *The students will* _____

Lesson #3. Describe briefly:

_____

_____

Rephrase in student behavior: *The students will* _____

Why is this a powerful way to plan and teach? Discuss your answer with a partner teacher.

_____

_____

_____

_____

_____

_____

_____

_____

_____

_____

Smile, Smile, Smile!: Classroom Solution/Strategy #37

Abundant smiles from a teacher throughout the day lead to fewer behavior problems.

What is:

For approximately what percent of your teaching day do you smile?

0-20%   21-40%   41-60%   61-80%   81-100%

If your response puts you at 60% of the time or less, explain what prevents you from smiling more. If you are at 61% or higher, explain what gives you cause to smile so often.

_____

_____

_____

What could be:

Mark T for True and F for False for the following statements.

_____ I studied and planned to become a teacher.

_____ I work hard and get paid for my work as a teacher.

_____ I make a difference in the lives of other human beings.

_____ I can influence decisions, outcomes, and events as a teacher.

_____ I never have the same day twice, so boredom is difficult to claim.

_____ Children and their parents look to me for guidance, support, ideas, and help.

_____ I work with other like-minded professionals toward a similar goal.

_____ I have numerous holidays and long vacations.

_____ The more I work in my profession and the more I learn about it, the more I get paid.

_____ I work with happy, motivated, and sometimes truly funny young people every day.

_____ I have lots of good reasons to be "a miserable teacher growing miserably old."

_____ People who smile a lot have luckier and happier lives than I do.

_____ I expect professionals I hire to be friendly and pleasant when they are working with me (doctor, nurse, hair stylist, dentist, customer service representative, auto mechanic, etc.).

_____ People who smile often usually continue to smile even when they do not receive smiles in return.

In addition to some of the reasons included in the list above, list eight more reasons you have to smile every day—in your professional or personal life (Ex: you are in good health, you have a loving family, etc.).

1. _____

2. _____

3. _____

4. _____

5. _____

6. _____

7. _____

8. _____

What is it that might be preventing you from smiling most of the time while you are teaching?

_____

_____

_____

If your answer is that you are truly unhappy about being a teacher right now or that you truly do not enjoy your students, what is the next step? What do you, your students, and your profession deserve?

_____

_____

Make it real:

The authors suggest several occasions during teaching when a smile can make a big difference. Rank these times in the list below according to the order in which you will begin to make a conscious effort to smile at your students on a daily basis.

_____   Greet my students.

_____   Begin my lesson with a smile.

_____   Encourage them with a smile as they work.

_____   Thank them with a smile whenever it is warranted.

_____   Smile at each one as they leave class.

Try it for one day! Smile until your face hurts! Smile all the time. During that day, jot down how you're feeling and what reactions you see in students. Notice how you feel at the end of the day. What comments did people/students make to you? Did you smile in the face of blank stares, ugly glares, unhappy faces, and moody eyes? How did that feel?

My Smile Journal

_____

_____

_____

_____

_____

_____

_____

_____

_____

_____

_____

_____

_____

_____

Teaching With Urgency:
Classroom Solution/Strategy #38

Convey each lesson's urgency, excitement, and importance to your students, and capture their attention.

What is:

Circle the words that a neutral observer would use to describe your typical lesson.

Engaging	*Stimulating*	*Interesting*	*Ho-Hum*	*Laborious*	*Dry*
Captivating	*Student-centered*	*Well-organized*	*Easy to follow*	*Surprising*	*Clever*
Different	*Unexpected*	*Typical*	*Traditional*	*Slow*	*Difficult*

What other words describe your teaching? (Be as honest and fair as possible.)

_____ _____ _____

_____ _____ _____

What could be:

Take a minute to remember an infomercial or sales channel on television that you have watched. What are the key characteristics that keep you drawn to watching and learning more, even if you have no intention of purchasing the product? Consider ways these infomercial descriptors could be transferred to teaching a lesson. For example:

Infomercial Characteristics	**Applied to My Teaching**
Highly visually appealing	*"I could plan my lessons to include more strong visuals for emphasis."*
Speaker looks directly at the camera, speaking to me	_____ _____

Clear sound, tone of warmth, and
excitement about product

_____

Repetitive message

_____

_____

Simple statements and descriptive
adjectives

_____

_____

Make you feel as if you *need* this
product

_____

_____

Make it real:

What are five specific skills, strategies, or behaviors *you* will use to convey urgency, importance, and excitement about your lesson content?

1. _____

2. _____

3. _____

4. _____

5. _____

Plan a "Teacher Infomercial" lesson this week. Practice and plan the details, language, introduction, and activities carefully. Incorporate key characteristics of infomercials and plan your own enthusiasm for the lesson. Then teach the lesson. What did you notice about your students' attention, responses, and mastery of the lesson content? Share your experiences, ideas, and outcomes with a partner who is trying the same approach.

My Infomercial Lesson is _____

I will show urgency by _____

_____

I will convey excitement by _____

_____

I will capture attention by _____

_____

I will repeat key phrases or words such as _____

_____

My visuals will include _____

_____

My body language will be _____

_____

Student activities will be _____

_____

And, _____

_____

And, _____

_____

To end the lesson (make the sale), I will _____

_____

_____

_____

_____

_____

_____

Make It Doable and Chewable: Classroom Solution/Strategy #39

Break each learning skill or behavior goal into intermediate steps so students can succeed and improve.

What is:

If a student in your class cannot write a sentence and you are teaching paragraph writing, do you include that student in your paragraph-writing activities? (Apply this idea to any subject area.) Explain what you do and why you choose to do that.

_____

_____

_____

Do you ensure that the tasks you give to your students are actually doable for them, or do you sometimes know in advance that several students will not be able to successfully complete a particular assignment? Explain.

_____

_____

_____

Even when a task is doable for all students, do you sometimes find that they get overwhelmed if you do not break it into smaller pieces?

_____

_____

_____

Do you sometimes just teach a lesson to the entire class, knowing that the lesson is above the levels of some of your students? Why or why not?

_____

_____

_____

What could be:

Discuss an activity you assigned where students felt overwhelmed. What could you have done differently to make it more doable and chewable for *all* students?

_____

_____

_____

_____

_____

_____

_____

The authors also suggest small, accomplishable steps to address student misbehaviors. Use the suggestions in the text to write a plan for those behavior issues. Add your own details or steps as well!

Goal: *I want Ellen to stop talking out of turn, but she's very impulsive and does it 20-30 times a day.*

Steps: _____

_____

_____

Goal: *I want to improve student attendance for the rest of the year. Right now, only two students have been here every day—and it's October!*

Steps: _____

_____

_____

Goal: *I need Joshua to remain in his seat doing work for at least 20 minutes during class. In 20 minutes right now, he gets up at least 8-10 times.*

Steps: _____

_____

_____

Make it real:

Consider your own students' academic skill needs and behavior needs. Develop a doable and chewable plan for one academic skill you will be teaching in an upcoming lesson. Develop plans for two behaviors you want to improve.

Academic skill or lesson goal: _____

    First I will _____

_____

    Then _____

_____

    Next _____

_____

    Next _____

_____

_____

Behavior goal: _____

    First I will _____

_____

    Then _____

_____

    Next _____

_____

    Next _____

_____

_____

Behavior goal: _____

First I will _____

_____

Then _____

_____

Next _____

_____

Next _____

_____

_____

Share your plans with a partner. Seek ideas and feedback for additional or missing steps that will build success, step by step.

How will you feel when your students succeed again and again as they strive toward a goal?

_____

_____

_____

_____

_____

_____

_____

_____

_____

_____

_____

_____

Brag About Them to Others: Classroom Solution/Strategy #40

Brag about students or tell them you bragged about them—and behavior improves.

What is:

Can you list six separate times you have bragged about your class and to whom?

I bragged about my class to _____ for _____.

I bragged about my class to _____ for _____.

I bragged about my class to _____ for _____.

I bragged about my class to _____ for _____.

I bragged about my class to _____ for _____.

Now list individual students you have bragged about to others for something they have done or for qualities they possess. Can you list six?

I bragged about _____ to _____ for
_____

I bragged about _____ to _____ for
_____

I bragged about _____ to _____ for
_____

I bragged about _____ to _____ for
_____

I bragged about _____ *to* _____ *for*

_____

I bragged about _____ *to* _____ *for*

_____

Was it difficult for you to list six in each of the two categories? Or, could you have listed even more if there was more space? Reflect on the answers to these questions and what they imply about your use of this strategy.

_____

_____

_____

Do you need to increase the regularity with which you make sure the children know you are bragging about them? What are your thoughts as you review your lists? To whom have you bragged? What have you bragged about? How have you let your students know that you have bragged about them? Are you lacking in your use of this strategy?

_____

_____

_____

_____

What could be:

List the first names of five of your students. Write something you could brag about regarding each.

Name	"Brag-able" Quality
_____	_____
_____	_____
_____	_____
_____	_____
_____	_____

Which people offer you opportunities to brag about your students? Add specific people in your school or community who are possibilities in addition to those suggested below:

♦ Teacher assistant who helps with a special needs student in my room

♦ Grade-level team colleagues near my room

♦ The reading specialist who works with some of my students

♦ The special education teacher who works with some of my students

♦ The principal

Other people:

_____   _____

_____   _____

_____   _____

Make it real:

Make a specific plan for your next week of teaching. List four things you will brag about regarding your class as a whole. List four things you will brag about regarding a specific student.

List four things you will brag about regarding one of your colleagues to another colleague, a parent, or the principal.

I will brag about my class doing …

1. _____ to _____

2. _____ to _____

3. _____ to _____

4. _____ to _____

I will brag about my student, _____, for _____

Name: _____ , for _____

Name: _____ , for _____

Name: _____ , for _____

Name: _____ , for _____

I will brag about my colleague, _____, for
_____

I will brag about my colleague, _____, for
_____

I will brag about my colleague, _____, for
_____

How does it make *you* feel when you brag lavishly about your students and colleagues?

_____

_____

_____

_____

The Diversion Excursion:
Classroom Solution/Strategy #41

Wise teachers cleverly divert a student's attention from an actual or potential problem.

What is:

When you are teaching and you see a problem that is about to erupt or has actually erupted, what do you do?

_____

_____

_____

_____

Describe an actual example of a classroom incident that came to mind as you considered how you handle these problem situations.

_____

_____

_____

_____

Did you handle this incident while remaining calm and positive, without engaging in a power struggle with the student? If so, great. If not, was your approach less than successful?

_____

_____

_____

_____

_____

_____

Do you use any diversion tactics in your teaching? The authors list a couple that many people use. Add to the list by discussing your bag of tricks with a colleague or two.

♦ Calling the child's name and diverting attention with a question or intriguing statement.

♦ Interrupting the behavior in process and asking the child to do something else.

♦ Offering a positive statement or compliment that catches the child off guard, distracting him/her.

♦ _____

♦ _____

♦ _____

What could be:

Read the classroom scenarios below. Write something you could do as a teacher to distract or divert the students and prevent a behavior problem from erupting.

Cassidy is the class busy body. She cannot stand to let others handle their own problems. Two students, Victoria and Katelyn, are mature young ladies and best friends who obviously had an argument just before coming into class. They are sending each other angry looks, tossing their heads, rolling eyes at each other, and so on. Most of the class is working fine and ignoring the two. You want to ignore it as well since it is a personal problem you are confident they will work out later. But Cassidy is intrigued. She is giving Victoria and Katelyn her full attention and whispering to them, "What's wrong, you guys? What happened?" Although the girls ignore her, Cassidy gets louder and starts to scoot her chair in their direction.

What can you do to divert Cassidy's attention away from the girls and get students focused on the lesson?

_____

_____

_____

_____

Lucy is easily self-distracted into daydreaming. Right now, she is sitting in her desk gazing out the nearby window and twirling her hair round and round her finger. Her pencil is in her other hand but she is mentally not even "in the room" during this his-

tory test. Lucy has a short fuse and gets upset easily. She loves to create drama in order to get everyone's attention. She is quick to point out the unfairness of people who call her to task for something she does wrong. Everyone is working quietly on the test.

How can you get Lucy's attention back to her test without disturbing the class or turning Lucy into an angry, dramatic person who will certainly interrupt the test session?

_____

_____

_____

_____

Make it real:

Now it is your turn. In the boxes below, describe two actual situations you have experienced in your classroom where things were headed for trouble. Trade your scenarios with a colleague or partner and solve each other's scenarios with a "distraction" strategy. Compare notes and discuss the "diversion excursion" strategies each of you developed.

Scenario 1: _____

_____

_____

Diversion strategy: _____

_____

_____

Scenario 2: _____

_____

_____

_____

Diversion strategy: _____

_____

_____

Change the Way They Think:
Classroom Solution/Strategy #42

Students will want *to learn* when we change their beliefs about learning and create relevant lessons.

What is:

List a common negative belief students often hold about the following topics:

Ex.: Math class, fractions unit: *"Fractions are really hard to understand. Math is dumb."*

Reading a chapter in social studies: _____

Taking notes during class: _____

Studying for a test: _____

Essay questions: _____

Reading: _____

P.E. (if one is not athletic): _____

Being pulled out for special education services: _____

Being pulled out for gifted services: _____

Homework: _____

Add two of your own to the above list.

_____

_____

Have you ever said something like, "You need to know this because it is important in life"? _____ If so, was it a convincing point that encouraged students?

_____

_____

What could be:

Select two of the negative beliefs listed on the previous page. Develop a relevant explanation or lesson for each. Do the same for your two examples. Experiment with ways to create interest and relevance for students.

Ex.: Math is dumb. *"Fractions are the basis of almost everything we do. You work with money in whole dollars and parts (quarters, halves, tenths, one hundredths, one twentieth). You divide dessert, pizza, sandwiches, and other foods into equal parts all the time. Baseball batting averages are really fractions! Let me show you how a .300 batting average is really the fraction 3/10 for three hits out of 10 tries."*

Negative Belief 1: _____

_____

_____

_____

_____

Your relevant explanation: _____

_____

_____

_____

_____

Negative Belief 2: _____

_____

_____

_____

_____

Your relevant explanation: _____

_____

_____

_____

_____

Make it real:

What will you say next time you hear ...

List three complaints you have recently heard from one or more of your students regarding work you asked them to do. Write your relevant response so you are prepared the next time you hear it. Help your students learn to think differently about these things.

Common Complaint #1: _____

Next time I hear that, I will say:

_____

_____

_____

_____

_____

Common Complaint #2: _____

Next time I hear that, I will say:

_____

_____

_____

_____

Common Complaint #3: _____

Next time I hear that, I will say:

_____

_____

_____

_____

_____

Nip It in the Bud:
Classroom Solution/Strategy #43

By taking care of minor behavior problems quickly, effective teachers rarely deal with serious ones.

What is:

List three situations in your class that have started as minor annoyances and become full-blown problems. Explain what happened for each and why you think these situations escalated.

Situation 1: _____

_____

_____

_____

_____

Situation 2: _____

_____

_____

_____

_____

Situation 3: _____

_____

_____

_____

_____

What could be:

1. List some actual serious behaviors you deal with from time to time in your teaching.
2. Indicate what less serious behaviors probably preceded these serious ones.
3. Finally, code your response to the less serious incident as follows:

    I = *I ignored it.*

    W = *It was not worth my time to address it.*

    N = *I dealt with it and nipped it in the bud.*

    S = *I did not see or know about it.*

Example:

Serious Behavior: *A big fight occurred at recess. Earlier that day in the hallway, Patrick bumped James just slightly. At recess, James called Patrick a loser when he let the other team score in soccer, so Patrick lost his temper, and a big fight ensued.*

Less serious incident that led to the problem: *The bump in the hall would have seemed like nothing to some. However, I know these two boys, and I had a feeling this could become a bigger problem.*

Code: **I** = *I saw it but just ignored it because we were running late and I had other things on my mind.*

♦ Serious Behavior: _____

_____

_____

Less serious incident that led to the problem:

Code: ____ = _____

♦ Serious Behavior: _____

_____

_____

Less serious incident that led to the problem:

Code: ____ = _____

Make it real:

Make a list of 10 relatively minor behaviors that have the potential to lead to serious problems. Write what you will say or do next time one of these minor behaviors occurs in your class so you can truly nip it in the bud.

Minor Behaviors:	*Next time I will …*
1. _____	_____
2. _____	_____
3. _____	_____
4. _____	_____
5. _____	_____
6. _____	_____
7. _____	_____
8. _____	_____
9. _____	_____
10. _____	_____

Share three of your 10 plans with a colleague. Did the two of you have some similar minor behaviors? Do you have some fresh ideas for how to nip the problems in the bud?

_____

_____

_____

_____

_____

_____

_____

_____

_____

_____

Discover the Beams of Their Dreams: Classroom Solution/Strategy #44

When a teacher makes it a point to know each child's dreams and goals, learning and behavior flourish.

What is:

List 15 of your students here. Beside their names, write what you know about that child's dreams and aspirations.

	Name:	*Dream or Aspiration*
1.		
2.		
3.		
4.		
5.		
6.		
7.		
8.		
9.		
10.		
11.		
12.		
13.		
14.		
15.		

Rate yourself by counting the number out of 15 whose goals and aspirations you knew.

If you knew the dreams and aspirations of …

♦ **12-15 students:** *You are amazing!* You likely have great relationships and few behavior problems. What do you do to get to know your students? Share your strategies with your colleagues.

_____

_____

♦ **8-12 students:** *You certainly have some good relationships!* Which students might you get to know better?

_____

_____

♦ **4-8 students:** *You do know a few.* Are they the "easy" ones? Those who readily share and talk about their experiences, dreams, and goals? How can you get to know all of your students well?

_____

_____

♦ **0-4 students.** *This is an important strategy for you to use.* You will like yourself, your students, and your work much better once you learn more about the fascinating young people you teach. What will you do to begin?

_____

_____

What could be:

Imagine you are a teacher who secretly dreams of acquiring a higher degree, but you have told no one. What might a supportive principal or coworker do or say differently if they knew about your dream?

Once one of these people (principal or coworker) knows your dream, how will you likely feel when they actively encourage, support, and help you to make it possible?

How much more likely will your dream be realized once you tell someone who is capable of helping you and supporting you on the path to realizing the dream?

How might your students react if you knew their dreams and encouraged them to achieve those dreams?

Make it real:

All of your students have dreams, ideas, goals, and aspirations. List eight strategies you will use in the weeks ahead to get to know your students' dreams and aspirations.

1. _____

2. _____

3. _____

4. _____

5. _____

6. _____

7. _____

8. _____

Work That Body Language: Classroom Solution/Strategy #45

Great teachers are always careful with their body language because they know it says much more than their words.

What is:

Match these body positions with their likely meaning:

1. Arms crossed over chest
2. Sitting back in chair, arms open
3. Leaning forward in chair, head tilted
4. Nervously standing fully erect and straight
5. Standing with knees slightly bent, arm leaning on the door
6. Sitting with legs crossed away from person you're in conversation with
7. Listening to someone, chin propped in hand, eyes closed, big sigh
8. Standing over someone, leaning forward talking to them

a. ____ Not interested in learning
b. ____ Comfortable and open, welcoming
c. ____ Listening carefully, open to what is being said and comfortable
d. ____ Intimidating and exerting power
e. ____ Listening carefully, thinking about what's being said
f. ____ Defensive and unwilling to engage honestly with the person
g. ____ Uncomfortable and bracing for the worst
h. ____ Pretending to listen, upset, and frustrated

(Best Answers: a = 6, b = 2, c = 3, d = 8, e = 3, f = 1, g = 4, h = 7)

Describe the body language you see from your students when they communicate these emotions during class (without saying a word).

Bored:

_____   _____

_____   _____

Interested:

_____   _____

_____   _____

Confused/Do not understand:

_____   _____

_____   _____

Nervous:

_____   _____

_____   _____

Just now "got it" (the concept you taught):

_____   _____

_____   _____

Worried or anxious (about the assignment or test):

_____   _____

_____   _____

Confident:

_____   _____

_____   _____

Have you ever, as the authors suggest, been accused of saying something to a child that you did not say? Briefly describe that incident:

_____

_____

_____

_____

Play the "video" of that incident again in your mind, watching your body language.

Is it possible you did say some things with your body language unintentionally or subconsciously?

What body language did you use that might have "said" those things?

_____

_____

_____

_____

_____

_____

_____

What could be:

You may be subconsciously sending unintended messages to your students with your body language.

The authors suggest a few ways to monitor or learn what body language you use. Which of their suggestions below would work best for you?

1. Focus on body language: Video yourself teaching and watch it privately with the sound off. What body messages did you send? Make a list of what you did with your hands, arms, stance, shoulders, expressions, tilt of head, sighs, and so on.

2. Focus on facial expressions: Video yourself teaching and watch it privately with the sound off. Focus only on your facial expressions. Count the smiles, frowns, times you made eye contact, mouth messages (grimace, pursed lips, biting lips, etc.).

3. Select a specific lesson in your day and monitor your body language. With your mind's eye, watch yourself teaching this lesson. Immediately after the lesson, write about what body language you used and what messages you sent. Consider what you might stop, start, or continue doing.

4. Invite a colleague to come and observe your teaching. Ask him/her to take objective and precise notes of only your body language and/or facial expressions by creating tallies for each expression, movement, and message conveyed. Analyze the data your colleague provides.

Make it real:

Select one of the strategies from the four above. Develop a specific plan to become more aware of your body language and the messages you are sending. Share your plan with a friend and plan to discuss the results with this person after you complete the experience.

Building My Body Language Awareness Plan

Which of the four experiences will you try from the list on the previous page?

When will you do it? Date: _____ Time: _____ Lesson/Class: _____

Why did you select that lesson/date/class? _____

How will you gather your data? _____

With whom will you discuss what you learned? _____

When? _____

Where? _____

No Rest for the Weary:
Classroom Solution/Strategy #46

It is a teacher's professional responsibility to be positive and fully engaged in quality work every day.

What is:

Circle the response that is true for you in each statement below.

♦ I come to work with a smile and positive attitude …

When I can, but it's hard …	Some of the time—on my good days	Much of the time unless …	Every day, no matter what, because it's my job

♦ I greet people when I arrive at work …

If I'm in a good mood	If they say "Hi" first	If I know them well	No matter what

♦ I teach with enthusiasm …

Not that often … I'm a bit burned out	When I have my bright and gifted students in class	Most of the time, but my energy wanes sometimes	Always, because I'm making a difference!

♦ As far as the problems with my school, department, principal and students, I …

Just have to throw up my hands	Talk a lot to others about what should be done	Work on committees and on my own to fix them	Look for and actualize solutions within my own sphere of influence

For your own children or children of family members, how would you want their teachers to respond to the above?

_____

_____

What could be:

Complete these statements.

When I am the best teacher I can be, I drive into the parking lot of school each morning thinking to myself _____

_____

When I am the best teacher I can be, I see my colleagues and say, _____

_____

When I am the best teacher I can be, my behavior in the classroom and elsewhere in the presence of students models _____

_____

When I am the best teacher I can be, I show enthusiasm for the subjects I teach by

_____

When I am the best teacher I can be, my negative thoughts and beliefs about others _____

_____

When I am the best teacher I can be, my exhaustion, weariness, and stress from my workload _____

_____

When I am the best teacher I can be, problems in the school or with my students or their families become opportunities for _____

_____

Make it real :

Rank the behaviors below, 1 indicating the area you most need to improve and 7 indicating an area you least need to improve in order to be a true professional.

_____ Putting a smile on my face every day, all day.

_____ Greeting everyone I meet kindly and warmly.

_____ Modeling appropriate behavior in the presence of my students.

_____ Approaching everything in my teaching —yes, everything—with enthusiasm.

_____ Never speaking negatively of anyone.

_____ Never complaining about my workload, colleagues, or students.

_____ Focusing my energy and attention on solutions, not problems.

Write assertive "I will" statements for the top three behaviors you need to change in order to become the best professional educator you can be.

I will _____

I will _____

I will _____

A Little Guilt Trip Goes a Long Way: Classroom Solution/Strategy #47

Expressing disappointment for misbehavior, as opposed to expressing anger, can help students to respond with remorse, not disdain.

What is:

Discuss these questions with a small group of colleagues.

◆ *What message do you send* to your students about your opinion of them when you respond to misbehavior with disappointment? _____

When you respond with anger? _____

◆ *What is the likely result* of helping your students to feel remorseful or guilty for their behavior? _____

When you provoke their anger or resentment? _____

What are three recent misbehaviors you have handled with
a student and/or class?   *Response

1. _____ _____

2. _____ _____

3. _____ _____

*For each incident, would you describe your response as:

   a. Expressing anger toward them
   b. Expressing disappointment in them

What could be:

Now *you* are the expert! Answer these teachers' questions about handling serious misbehavior. Explain how to use the guilt trip strategy to address the problem.

Dear Expert Teacher,

My students were playing football after school yesterday when two students started to argue about whether a player's foot was in or out of bounds. The argument quickly escalated until pushing led to fists flying between two students. The rest of my class stopped their play and circled around the two angry students to watch the fight. Seven or eight children joined in the fight, attacking classmates on the other team. I am appalled and shocked! We have been talking about this very thing almost every day and planning together what to do if a fight starts. What shall I say to my students when I see them today?

Signed, B. Wildered

Dear B. Wildered,

_____

_____

_____

_____

_____

Dear Expert Teacher,

I gave my students a history exam yesterday covering our WWII unit. I scored the exams during my lunch break and was so pleased with the excellent scores! Then I found out from another teacher who overheard some students talking in the cafeteria that a group of about eight students had cheated. I'm so angry with them for this dishonesty! What shall I say to them tomorrow? And what should the punishment be for this outrageous behavior?

Signed, Mr. N. Censed

Dear Mr. N. Censed,

_____

_____

_____

_____

_____

Discuss with your colleagues what aspects of a teacher's response make the difference between guilt trip and humiliation. Use the two scenarios on the previous page to discuss a guilt-based approach and a humiliation-based approach.

Fighting over soccer incident:

Guilt trip would be _____

_____

Humiliation would be _____

Cheating on history test:

Guilt trip would be _____

Humiliation would be _____

Make it real:

Select one of the three misbehaviors you identified in your own class at the beginning of this lesson.

Incident: _____

A good guilt trip response: _____

An inappropriate humiliation response: _____

As a final point, the authors emphasize that it is *not* effective to overuse the guilt trip strategy. They also imply that an angry response is *never* effective. What are some other strategies you have learned for responding to misbehavior? Did they work? Why or why not?

_____

_____

_____

_____

_____

_____

_____

Teach Them to Cope or They'll Create a Way!
Classroom Solution/Strategy #48

Explicitly teach coping skills and stress management techniques, and your student behavior problems will decrease.

What is:

Rate your students in the following coping-skill areas:

	Poor	Inadequate	Adequate	Skilled
Using please and thank you	1	2	3	4
Giving a genuine and articulate apology	1	2	3	4
Appropriately joining a conversation	1	2	3	4
Asking permission to join a game or group	1	2	3	4
Taking a breath and calming down instead of reacting angrily	1	2	3	4
Accepting an apology graciously	1	2	3	4
Using appropriate eye contact	1	2	3	4
Making a request with assertiveness and grace	1	2	3	4
Admitting to a mistake or expressing regret	1	2	3	4
Politely asking someone to stop something that is irritating or annoying or harmful	1	2	3	4
Using "I-statements" to ask for what is needed	1	2	3	4
Responding effectively if called a name or teased	1	2	3	4
Responding skillfully if threatened	1	2	3	4

Introducing oneself or others to a new person	1	2	3	4
Rate your efforts for teaching these skills to your students	1	2	3	4
Rate your school's culture for teaching, expecting, and modeling these skills for students	1	2	3	4

What could be:

Have you ever considered the basic parts of a sincere apology?

1. Make eye contact.
2. Say the person's name.
3. State *"I am sorry for* _____ . *I shouldn't have* _____ . *Next time I will* _____ . *Please accept my apology."*
4. Extend your hand for a handshake.

And the appropriate response to an apology?

1. Make eye contact.
2. Say, *"Thank you,* _____ *(name). I accept your apology."*
3. Accept the offer to shake hands if willing to do so.

If you teach and expect this simple skill from your students, what might be the result?

_____

_____

What are the steps or social rules for joining a conversation or activity with a group? Describe the socially acceptable things to say and do in order to join a group.

_____

_____

One common and effective way to teach and practice coping skills is through *role play,* dramatizing things the wrong way and then the right way. How can you incorporate this strategy into your teaching?

_____

_____

Make it real:

From the list of coping skills you rated above, select one where you believe your students are lacking because they have not been taught. List the steps or ways you will teach the skill. Share your results with a partner.

Critical Coping Skill:

What I need to teach about this skill:

1. _____

2. _____

3. _____

4. _____

A lesson or approach I will use to teach this skill to my students:

_____

_____

_____

_____

_____

_____

_____

_____

Ways I can incorporate this skill into my classroom expectations, positive behavior rewards system, and classroom culture:

_____

_____

_____

_____

_____

_____

Listen, Listen, Listen!
Classroom Solution/Strategy #49

Teachers who use skillful listening strategies enable their students to express and solve problems.

What is:

To whom do you go when you have a problem? _____

_____

What listening skills do you notice about that person when you are sharing your problem? _____

_____

How do you feel after spending time sharing your problem with a good listener?

_____

How do you believe your students would rate YOU regarding your listening skills?

Not a good listener   *A fairly good listener*   *An excellent listener*

What could be:

Listening is a valuable skill. It serves teachers well in their work with children. But how can it also add quality to all relationships in one's life? _____

_____

Work with a partner to respond to the following questions. Refer to the numerous listening strategies in the book as well as your own experience as a listener.

Describe the body language of a good listener. _____

_____

_____

Describe the words of a good listener. _____

_____

_____

When someone with a problem is skillfully listened to, a solution usually evolves. Should it be the listener or the speaker who most often identifies the solution? Why?

_____

_____

_____

Make it real:

Try it! Take turns listening and speaking with a partner. Tell your partner a story about a humorous or embarrassing incident from childhood. Use lots of detail and make it a great story. Talk while your partner listens and says *nothing*. Then you listen and say nothing while your partner tells his/her story.

As the speaker,

♦ What did you notice about yourself as you talked? _____

_____

♦ How did it feel to have someone so focused on your story? _____

_____

♦ What did the listener do that you liked? _____

_____

As the listener,

♦ What did you notice as you listened? _____

_____

_____

♦ Were you really listening or were you thinking about something else instead? What was going on in your head?_____

_____

♦ Was it difficult to stay completely focused on the person speaking? If so, how could you improve your ability to do this?_____

_____

♦ Could your partner tell if you were truly listening and when you were pretending to listen? _____

_____

Now take time to experience an expanded, high-quality version of listening, speaking, and problem solving. This time tell your partner about a genuine *problem* you are having—any problem at all.

♦ Take 2 minutes to talk about the problem.

♦ After you describe the problem, your listener will begin to use *very few words* such as, *"I'm listening"* or *"Tell me more about …"*

♦ After you have clarified and given details about your problem, the listener should paraphrase what s/he's heard without offering a solution. You can clarify or add details.

♦ Finally, the listener can say something like, *"So what might be the best thing for you to do first?"*

♦ As speaker, you will probably notice yourself automatically starting to come up with ideas for solutions as you begin to clarify and explain the problem. It is remarkable and very satisfying.

♦ In 5-10 minutes with a good listener, you will likely have some good ideas to start solving the problem, and all your partner did was listen and ask questions. Switch roles and listen to your partner's problem.

How will this type of listening skill be helpful with your students?

_____

_____

_____

_____

Only a Fool Loses His Cool:
Classroom Solution/Strategy #50

Promise your students you will never raise your voice with them or berate them. Then live up to the commitment.

What is:

1. How many screamers can you name (to yourself) among the staff at your school?
   _____

2. Might your name come up on someone else's list of screamers? _____
   If no, that is great, but do you sometimes lose your cool with students?

   _____

3. What does a screamer model for his/her students?_____

   _____

4. What does it say about the screamer? _____

   _____

5. Do you believe doctors, customer service people, police, emergency medical teams, or receptionists ever get their buttons pushed as hard as students might push yours? _____

6. How do you expect these people to behave when working with you? _____

   _____

7. Are you ever a button pusher with people in other professional roles? _____

   _____

8. When someone loses his cool with you, despite his professional role, what do you then believe about that person or company (even when you did push the buttons)?

   _____

What could be:

The authors suggest making a promise to your students about what you will expect from them and then what they can expect from you—specifically that you will *not* raise your voice in anger at them.

Could you make such a promise?

> *Easily   Maybe   No, I am not ready to do that*

How easy will it be for you to keep this promise?

> *Not a problem   Since I promised,   It will be difficult, but   Hard to do—*
> *   I'll stick to it   with practice I'll improve   doubt myself*

Make it real:

Students will continue to push your buttons, regardless of any promise you make or expectations you set for them. To avoid letting them get to you, first you must know your buttons.

Make a list of your "Teacher Buttons." Some suggestions are listed to get you started.

Possible Buttons:

> *talking back   rolling eyes   profanity   apathy   insincerity*
>
> *sarcasm   yelling   nervous   profane   cynical*
> *   behaviors   gestures   retorts*

My buttons:

_____   _____

_____   _____

_____   _____

_____   _____

Select the three that really cause you to lose your cool. Make a plan for a new approach you will use next time those buttons get pushed by one or more students.

My button: _____

My new behavior when this button is pushed: *I will* _____

_____

_____

_____

My button: _____

My new behavior when this button is pushed: *I will* _____

_____

_____

_____

My button: _____

My new behavior when this button is pushed: *I will* _____

_____

_____

_____

If you enjoyed this book, we recommend:

What Great Teachers Do *Differently*

14 Things That Matter Most

Todd Whitaker

"This book is easy to read and provides essential information.
I've ordered copies for every one of my teachers."

—*Ann Ferell, Principal*
Autrey Mill Middle School, GA

What if all your teachers could be just like the best teachers?

This book focuses on the specific things that great teachers do that others do not. It describes the beliefs, behaviors, attitudes, and interactions that form the fabric of life in our best classrooms and schools.

What Great Teachers Do Differently answers these essential questions—

- Is it high expectations for students that matter?
- How do great teachers respond when students misbehave?
- Do great teachers filter differently than their peers?
- How do the best teachers approach standardized testing?
- How can your teachers gain the same advantages?

2004, 144 pp. paperback 669-1 $29.95 plus shipping and handling

Also available—

Study Guide: What Great Teachers Do
Differently: 14 Things that Matter Most

Beth Whitaker and Todd Whitaker

2006, 96 pp. paperback 7024-X $16.95 plus shipping and handling

Save $$$ on multiple copy orders!
To order and for details, contact Eye On Education at
888-299-5350 or www.eyeoneducation.com

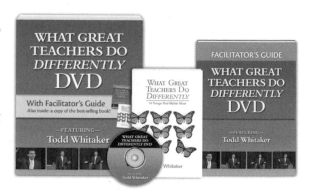